The Feminization of the Church?

Kaye Ashe

Sheed & Ward
Kansas City

Sheed & Ward™ is a service of The National Catholic Reporter Publishing Company.

Library of Congress Cataloging-in-Publication Data:
Ashe, Kaye.
    The feminization of the church? / Kaye Ashe.
        p.   cm.
    Includes bibliographical references.
    ISBN 1-58051-028-0 (alk. paper)
    1. Women in the Catholic Church. 2. Feminism—Re
        ligious aspects—Christianity. I. Title
BX2347.8.W6A73 1997
282'.082—dc21
                                                    97-41160
                                                    CIP

Published by: Sheed & Ward
               115 E. Armour Blvd.
               P.O. Box 419492
               Kansas City, MO 64141-6492.

To order, call: (800) 333-7373

www.natcath.com.sheedward

This book is printed on recycled paper.
Cover design by Biner Design.

Contents

In loving memory of Sr. Albertus Magnus McGrath, O.P., teacher and mentor, who challenged women to use their intelligence, instinct, hearts, and daring to transform church and society.

Acknowledgments

I want to acknowledge first and with immense gratitude the Sinsinawa Dominicans, whose support made possible the time and research necessary for the writing of this book. I am grateful, too, to the administration of the Jesuit School of Theology at Berkeley for granting me the privileges attendant upon Visiting Scholar status. One of those privileges was the use of the library of the Graduate School of Theology, whose staff was unfailingly courteous and helpful.

Numerous family members and friends offered encouragement and useful suggestions that have enhanced the text. I wish to thank them all, and in particular my Dominican sisters Joan O'Shea, Marilyn Aiello, Catherine Dooley, Candida Lund and Anne Marie Mongoven. I am equally grateful to Mary Jo Chavez, Mary DeLargy, Patricia Brommel, Elizabeth Cotter, Marta Vides, and Siddika Angle, who read and commented on various chapters. Ann McCullough, O.P. read the entire manuscript, investing her time and skill in the enhanced readability of the text. My warmest thanks go also to Nora Schaefer, O.P., who read the manuscript, honed my computer skills, helped prepare the final copy, and aided in other ways too numerous to mention.

Foreword

Joan Chittister, O.S.B.

The French philosopher Blaise Pascal wrote three centuries ago what may well be the real effect of a book like this. He said, "It is true that force rules the world, but opinion looses force." It is an ominous insight. It rings with a clamorous truth. When the credibility of an institution is eroded, the power of the institution disintegrates. Only the skeleton of force remains. Only the ability to restrict continues to operate in that system. Its ability to energize, people discover one morning, has been long gone. Then the signs of such change appear everywhere. Public criticism begins. Internal dissension erupts. The institution dies from the inside out.

At the same time, such places seldom disappear. They may stay in place, ghosts of their former selves, sites of some kind of private and pious consolation, perhaps, but for all practical purposes stripped of effect in the public arena. They simply lose their power to influence.

But if that is true, and social history is rife with the bones of once-vibrant systems now defunct – monarchies leveled, econcomic systems felled, religions reduced to the level of quaint custom – then at this very moment there are termites in the foundation of the Roman Catholic Church. Where more and more women are concerned, the church has lost its claim to moral purity. And they are saying so. Some stay in the church for love of the tradition, but without respect for the structure. Some stay in the church, but worship with women's groups as well. Many of them have left the church already, never to be seen again – part of other faiths now or of no faith at all. Those who return to the church, if they ever do, come back in most part for the sake of their children, for whom they seek a sacramental life but whose catechesis they edit. Parents, mothers have become the teachers of Catholic education, and for a growing number that translates as a responsibility to mount a clear and confident contradiction of canons and practices and moral instructions based on the the inferiority of women, the inequality of the sexes, and the invisibility of women in the church. They debate such subjects in the presence of their chidren. They answer questions more out of disquiet than out of heart. "Mama, why are there no girl-priests in our church?" the small daughter of a Canadian couple demanded to know one Sunday morning after Mass. "Because," her parents answered, uncomfortable at having to deal so early with the question they knew would someday be inevitable, "our church doesn't allow girl-priests. Yet." "Then," the little girl asked, astonished, "why do we go there?"

Parents don't correct attitudes like that anymore. On the contrary, they themselves are cautioning their children against accepting such positions without qualification, without reservation. They are admitting their own discomfort, their own confusion, their own rejection of ideas that defy the liberating message of the Gospel. They pronounce such things downright wrong and make a distinction for their children between the faith, the tradition, the gospel, and the institution. That kind of catechesis builds another church in the shell of the old one.

In the face of such public misgiving, to stem the tide of doubt, letters of condemnation and "clarification" are pouring out of church bureaucracies. Theologians are being

silenced. Organizations bent on discussion, change or renewal in the church are being threatened. People are being
condemned. Petitions are being ignored. But nothing
changes. The stream of thought in contradiction to official
positions continues to flow out of journals, books, academic
consultations, and popular magazines, despite the disap-
proval, despite all injunctions to the contrary. The people
are bent on being heard. It is a new church, whether anyone
wants it to be new or not.

No such questioning, no such emendations, no such
doubt, no such independence in the faith life could ever
have happened in my childhood.

Women are speaking out everywhere, talking back,
speaking up, straightening their shoulders and responding
to the issues, despite the fact that they have not been asked
the questions. In that sense, then, the church has already
been "feminized."

What is lacking, of course, is the inclusion of women in
the structures of the church itself, not as tokens or as
observers but as members, as authorities, as ministers, as
women. Indeed, the dualism still exists. The only difference
now is that this time it comes wearing a smiling face. It
says, "We're sorry," and then it says "But we can't help it."
It says, "You're human," and then it says, "But a very special
kind of human." Which, translated, means "not a male
human," another kind of human: "unique," "special," "different." Too unique, too special, too different to be really
what was incarnated, really what was fully baptized, defi-
nitely full of grace, or genuinely created in the image of
God, regardless of what God had to say about it.

The problem is that fewer and fewer people every
day believe such things. Pascal's insight takes on a current
color. "It is true that force rules, but opinion looses force"
becomes more warning than insight. Kaye Ashe's *The Feminization of the Church?* pinpoints the erosion that even now

haunts and torments, stalks and troubles the church. It bells the cat, it sounds the alarm. It records under one cover the slow, slow process that is changing the face of humankind. It is an important vein to follow because it marks a stepover point in history, a cataclysm of changing perspective reminiscent of the Reformation in its immensity. The new awaeness seeps like lava through fissures in a rock. It cannot be held back. It is the feminization of human consciousness.

What *The Feminization of the Church?* does not actually say but at the same time says only too clearly is its most serious message. It is only a matter of time now before the Church is really whole – or really redundant.

Joan Chittister, O.S.B.

Introduction

When, in the course of writing this book, I would tell interested parties its title, I met with a variety of reactions. One was incredulity: "Have I missed something?" A "feminized" church was still beyond the reach of imagination. A nephew, willing to grant that *something* was changing, but realizing things hadn't changed all that much, wisecracked, "Oh, so it's going to be a *short* book." Others are suspicious of the term "feminized," and with reason. If we associate the term with "feminine," by which we mean all that is perfumed, powdered, dainty and dull, or wily, seductive, manipulative and powerless, we might well be strongly opposed to feminizing anything – least of all girls. Indeed, many feminists argue that to feminize or to masculinize children is to warp them. And when the terms are understood in the framework of stereotypical gender traits, I couldn't agree more. Along these same lines, some fear that using the term "feminization" tends to tame things or to mask certain realities. Thus, the editors of the book *For Crying Out Loud: Women and Poverty in the United States* ask, "Did the long-needed naming of the problem as the *feminization* of poverty . . . tend to put a pink dress on issues that were somehow more serious when they affected men?"[1] They prefer the straightforward term "the impoverishment of women."

In another context, Ann Douglas, in her justly acclaimed *Feminization of American Culture*, uses the term "feminization" to describe the sentimentalization of both the theological and secular cultures in the United States of the 19th century. With the disestablishment of the Protestant churches, literate ministers, deprived of public support and a role in public affairs, turned to women and the domestic sphere. Here they found the sensibility, meekness, poverty of spirit, and sheer goodness that would serve as an antidote to the raw power of an America pushing toward expansion, urbanization and industrialization. In concert, ministers, white middle-class women and popular writers set out to save society with their emphasis on feeling, nurture, generosity, receptivity, and gentleness. Their effort, according to Douglas, served not to strengthen authentically matriarchal values but to intensify sentimental ones, and to sound the death knell of authentic Calvinism. She does not mourn the demise of the Calvinist faith. It was, however great, ". . . repressive, authoritarian, dogmatic, patriarchal to an extreme." [2] But, she contends, it deserved more worthy opponents. The ones who brought it down failed to replace it with a viable, sexually diversified culture. Furthermore, with their emphasis on the subliminal aspects of faith, rather than on its potential as a tool for protest, the sentimentalists became a conservative force limiting the possibilities for change in American society. Thus, while gutting Calvinism of its finest values, the feminization of American culture at the same time assured ". . . the continuation of male hegemony in different guises."[3]

In Douglas' understanding of the term, then, the feminization of a church or culture has a crippling rather than a liberating effect. But Douglas herself sometimes puts the words "feminization" or "feminizing" in quotation marks, signalling, I believe, her realization that the term has multiple meanings. The meaning I attach to the phrase "the feminization of the church" has to do, not with the kind of feminine culture that Douglas describes (one of genteel passivity that critiques patriarchal structures while capitulating to them), but with the effect on the church of a raised, feminist consciousness.

Christine E. Gudorf accepts Douglas' use of the term "feminization" in her analysis of the feminization of religion from the Roman Catholic viewpoint.[4] In her view, the church lost status and credibility in the political realm when it protested the scientific discoveries and the rule of the scientific method that began in the 16th century. This protest caused faith, in the secular mind, to be dissociated from reason, the preeminently masculine faculty that ordered society and civilization, and to be identified with the emotional and intuitive, that is, with the feminine and the domestic sphere. A number of historical circumstances converged to push Roman Catholicism even further from the center of an evolving, secular culture and into a defiantly defensive position, intensifying the trend toward the centralization of authority and tightening the demand for unquestioning obedience among Catholics. While the hierarchy, as a result, continued to be viewed as authoritarian and masculine, church members came to be viewed as subservient and obedient, that is, feminine. Gudorf continues her analysis by illustrating how the church, distanced from the liberal governments that were in power in Europe, turned its attention to marriage and the family, sexuality, and the education of children, strengthening the impression that religion was a domestic affair. Numerous papal tracts served to identify women as keeper of the hearth and guardian of religion and morals, and men as shapers of the world of public affairs. The challenge of Vatican II was to move the church from the private, feminine sphere to the masculine, public one, thereby restoring the church's voice in the world of political and corporate action. Gudorf's basic thesis is that the move from the private to the public sphere will not succeed unless the church tends to the feminine/masculine split in its own house, and allows the laity the autonomy that is required if they are to function as an evangelizing and humanizing force in the world. She finds in feminist theory a means of healing the public/private, masculine/feminine, clerical/lay, celibate/sexually active, and powerful/powerless divisions that continue to plague the church and rob it of its effectiveness as a builder of community and a bearer of the Good News of peace, freedom and justice.

It is my intention in this book to examine further the potential of feminist analysis to bring the church and its members to greater wholeness. I will not, as Gudorf does, look upon feminist theory as a means of recovery from the church's "feminization." I will see it rather as a means of effecting the feminization of the church understood as the full inclusion of women in the life of the church. The church becomes feminized in this sense when women exercise their right and ability to join in the human and religious activities of symbol-making, becoming not only consumers but creators of religious culture. It becomes feminized when women add their voices to the discourse on Christian ethics and claim their authority as responsible moral agents. Church language becomes feminized when it recognizes women's existence, experience, history and value; and ministry undergoes a feminization when every form of it is open to women. Finally, leadership in the church becomes feminized when it values relationship, inclusiveness, participation and flexibility, qualities that women's social experience has prepared them to value.

These are the issues treated in the chapters of this book. The question mark appears in the title for two reasons. First, because the process of feminization as I have described it here is far from complete; there are still forces within the church that resist every move to fully recognize and empower women. And secondly, because as we have seen, the term is open to several different interpretations.

John W. Glaser uses the term in a way similar to the way I intend it in this book in an article entitled "Epoch III: the church feminized."[5] Glaser embroiders here on Karl Rahner's thesis of the beginning of a third epoch of church history, which Rahner labels the World Church. This church succeeds Epoch I, a short period of Jewish Christianity, and Epoch II, the European Church which spanned two millennia. The forces of world culture will reshape and replace what Glaser describes as the ". . . slow, bountiful development of a European/Western Christianity."[6] Glaser expands on Rahner's thesis by pointing out that Epoch II was not only European, but also relentlessly male, and that Epoch III is destined to become a church of both women and men. He calls for ecclesiastical affirmative action to move us beyond not only the cultural but also the sexual colonialism of Epoch II. In regard to women, he states that this is necessary because ". . . the *injustices* are grave; the *wisdom and humanity lost* to our community are colossal."[7] Without pretending to predict how the full inclusion of women will affect the church, he suggests that women will bring to it an experience different from that of men in areas such as: ". . . community, ambiguity, body, power, symbol, violence . . . nurturance, sex, law . . . service."[8]

Both Rahner's thesis and Glaser's expansion of it give evidence that thinking people are aware that massive cultural shifts are occurring all around us, affecting the way we live, the thoughts we think, the language we use, the way we relate, and the myths and symbols we once cherished. These shifts are rooted in a complex of intersecting factors, not the least of which is a growing awareness that the patriarchal structures that have dictated the ways we live and relate have outgrown their usefulness and have become, in fact, intolerable to many and ultimately destructive to all.

Feminism is one of the social forces challenging patriarchy. Initially, feminists were engaged in a detailed and devastating critique of male domination and its effects on human development, but gradually their emphasis shifted to an analysis and valorization of women's way of knowing, feeling, relating, praying, leading, and arriving at moral decisions. And as the voices of women of various cultural, economic, racial and ethnic backgrounds joined the conversation, the white, middle-class feminists of the "First World" began to realize that there is not one correct way for women to know, think, feel and relate. In the ongoing conversation among women, and between women and men, it has become increasingly evident that much is to be gained by giving free rein in church and society to women's diverse gifts, creativity, and energy. A new vision is taking shape, a vision whose contours bear the mark of women's minds, hearts and aspirations.

While it is clear that patriarchy has not buckled in the face of this alternative vision, we can see signs (however feeble) of the feminization of certain public sectors: trades and professions, sports, politics, business, and the media, at least in the sense that women's presence in these arenas is no longer a novelty. An authentic feminist vision does not aim, however, at simply gaining leverage for women in an essentially unchanged patriarchal system. Feminism seeks to replace exclusionary and exploitative structures with ones based on principles of justice, reciprocity, and inclusion. The question to be explored in the pages that follow is the extent to which we can speak of the feminization of the church, that is, the extent to which the feminist vision is affecting church life. Because of my background and experience, the emphasis is on the Catholic church, but my conversations and interaction with women of all religious denominations convince me that we have much in common in terms of our frustrations, hopes, and aspirations. And while mine is a voice coming from a white, middle-class milieu, I hope the effect on me of multiple voices from other cultural contexts, and my debt to them, will be evident in the pages that follow.

Endnotes

1. Rochelle Lefkowitz and Ann Withorn, eds., *For Crying Out Loud: Women and Poverty in the United States* (New York: The Pilgrim Press, 1986), 4.
2. Ann Douglas, *The Feminization of American Culture* (New York: Doubleday, Anchor Book Edition, 1988), 13.
3. *Ibid.*
4. See her article "Renewal or Repatriarchal Roman Catholic Church to the Feminization of Religion," in *Horizons on Catholic Feminist Theology*, eds. Joann Wolski Conn and Walter E. Conn (Washington, D.C.: Georgetown University Press, 1992), 61-83.
5. *Commonweal*, 28 January 1983, 44-45.
6. *Ibid.*, 44.
7. *Ibid.*, 45.
8. *Ibid.*

Chapter 1

Women and Spirituality

What is Spirituality?

The term "spirituality" has become current coin in the religious vocabulary of Americans. In the world of scholarship, academic programs have sprung up to trace its development in the traditions of East and West. At the popular level, hundreds of books and artifacts are at our disposal, offering to acquaint us with the theories, methods and practice of spiritualities ranging from Eastern and traditional Christian to Native American and New Age. People flock to retreat centers and meditation centers in order to find or recover sources of hope, energy and inner peace. This turn to the spirit seems to be inspired in part by disillusionment with the frenetic accumulation of material things and the pace and stress necessary to acquire them. Weary of this unsatisfying search, and frightened by the isolation, competition and violence that mark our age, increasing numbers are looking within and beyond themselves for spiritual sustenance and the means, perhaps, to humanize the world as we approach the third millennium.

Until relatively recently, Catholics tended to use terms like "the interior life," "faith life," or "the spiritual life" rather than "spirituality." All of these terms refer to the ways we think, feel and act in respect to God or the Ultimate Good.

They point to an effort to attain self-fulfillment in the very act of transcending self and seeking loving union with God, others, and all God has created. Anne Carr observes, "Spirituality is larger than a theology or set of values precisely because it is all-encompassing and pervasive. Unlike theology as an explicit intellectual position, spirituality reaches into our unconscious or half-conscious depths."[1]

We speak in the Catholic tradition of various types of spiritualities: biblical spirituality, for instance, or the spirituality of the Desert Fathers, or that of the great religious orders – Benedictine, Franciscan, Dominican, Carmelite, Jesuit. Our spirituality may be affected by any of these sources. At the same time, it is shaped by our ethnic background, class, race and, yes, by our gender.

Since the spiritual search is fundamentally a human one, we may be reluctant to introduce the dimension of gender. Gender apparently has no significance in that realm where we encounter the Ultimate, but the fact is that *all* experience, including religious experience, is gendered. Without subscribing to the notion that men and women are essentially different (and by nature unequal), most people agree that in general, and for whatever reasons, there is a difference in the way women and men approach reality and relationships. The difference is expressed in various ways, and it affects the way men and women enter into the realm of the sacred. Men (at least in the dominant culture), tend to value analysis, definition, and the setting and achieving of goals; women tend to put greater emphasis on synthesis, understanding and process. Men are more at ease with the abstract; women are likely to translate abstract concepts into concrete reality. The latter prefer to combine head and heart knowledge, and are more aware of their own and others' feelings. Men, in the popular imagination, are associated with the "lofty" reaches of spirit and ideas, and work in the public arena; women are associated with body, and work in the "humble" arenas of the domestic and the earth-bound. Men seek independence; women prefer the interdependence required of reciprocal relationships. Neither men nor women are trapped in boxes with these labels, of course; and we can appreciate the worth of both sets of traits. Indeed, men and women alike should seek some balance and wholeness by becoming capable of the whole range of gifts and skills that the traits suggest.

The fact is, however, that the set attributed to men has historically been assigned greater value than the set attributed to women. Men, since the firm establishment of patriarchy, that is, for the past 5,000 years, have had greater status and authority in virtually every realm, including the realm of the spiritual. With some exceptions, and notably a few medieval mystics, women faced suspicion, interrogation, hostility, and even persecution when they attempted to communicate publicly their spiritual insights. Furthermore, women were denied access to the kind of education that would equip them to speak or write confidently of their experiences. Consequently, spiritual literature through much of history has been the domain of men, and bears the mark of a male perspective and a male approach to the world of the spirit. Some women, nevertheless, did write; and the last wave of the women's movement, together with renewed interest in women's history, affective prayer, and creation spirituality have brought these women to light.

Without absurdly exaggerating the differences between the spiritualities of men and women in the past, it will be useful to highlight some figures, male and female, in order to indicate, if only superficially, some distinctive marks of their commerce with God and with things of the spirit. This will serve to situate the current burgeoning of feminist spirituality, a spirituality grounded in women's new sense of self and in the conviction that the divine lives at their own center. Women's changed sense of self and of self-in-relation, their newly-won confidence in their power to name their own spiritual experience, affects not only women, but all of the circles in which they move. It changes everyone's understanding of the life of the spirit because it introduces into that arena voices that have been muffled or ignored and experiences that have been invisible or undervalued. The history of spirituality is enriched by the rediscovery, close study and wider dissemination of the writings of women from the past and the future of the life of the spirit looks much brighter, much fuller, much more exciting because of the continued exploration by women into their self-defined spiritual quest.

Some Spiritual Classics

A brief consideration of the spirituality of the Desert Fathers, of Thomas à Kempis, and of Ignatius of Loyola will serve to exemplify writings that have had enormous influence on the interior life of generations of Christians. Their writings are spiritual classics, and it would be foolish to deny that they have nourished both men and women through the ages. Nevertheless, there are in their writings assumptions, images and metaphors that are decidedly uncongenial to women. Their understanding of what constitutes spiritual health and growth often enough runs contrary to women's spontaneous experience of body, nature and society. We will consider first the spirituality of the Desert Fathers and Mothers.

Desert Spirituality

The sayings of the Desert Fathers (and the lesser-known Desert Mothers, to whom we shall return) contain passages of simple wisdom and touching compassion. Who can remain unmoved by the story of Abba Poemen who, when asked by some old men what they should do when they see brothers who are dozing during prayer, answered, "For my part, when I see a brother who is dozing, I put his head on my knees and let him rest."[2] The monks were sensitive to human frailty and unswerving in their search for God; they rejoiced in God's love and responded to it with the whole of their being. There is still much we have to learn from them.

Feminist thought in the past 20 years has, nevertheless, made it impossible to ignore the fact that the Desert Fathers and Fathers of the Church were steeped in misogyny and in the dualistic thinking that pitted heaven against earth, grace against nature, spirit against body, mind against emotion, and man against woman. Woman, associated with earth, nature, body and feeling, the "inferior" pole of each of the aforementioned pairs, was seen principally as a source of temptation. Basically evil, her surest path to salvation lay in "becoming a man." This strange transformation would take place with the help of a man's guidance and through a punishing kind of asceticism.

The ideal of the 3rd-century desert monks in Egypt, Syria and Palestine was to reclaim their true nature, conceived of as pure intellect, and to relentlessly mortify the flesh. Bodily functions were despised: eating, sleeping, sexual intercourse – all were considered inimical to the life of the spirit. Abba Bessarion is quoted as saying, "For fourteen days and nights, I have stood upright in the midst of thorn-bushes, without sleeping." And again, "For fourteen years I have never lain down, but have always slept sitting or standing."[3]

Quotations could be multiplied that reveal a seeming obsession with women's beauty and charm, and the monks' futile attempts to rid themselves of sexual fantasies. Abba Daniel, when asked by a brother for a commandment, replied, "Never put your hand in the dish with a woman, and never eat with her; thus you will escape a little the demon of fornication."[4] Women, the world, the flesh, and the devil were enemies to be fled and vanquished by the most extreme measures: throwing oneself into thorn bushes, denying oneself food, living in cisterns and atop pillars.[5] Spiritual enlightenment was bought at the price of self-denial and even self-abnegation.

Women willing to pay this price were allowed to join the desert monks. Lives of converted harlots, among whom the most famous were Pelagia, Maria, Thais, and Mary of Egypt, circulated among the monks, who found in these women some hope that their own habits of lust could be conquered.[6] The stories of these women are not biographies as such; in some cases they seem to be composite portraits, but there is no doubt that historical figures gave rise to the tales. Benedicta Ward, an Anglican religious and scholar, points out that the harlots were beautiful, rich, and free. They were constrained neither by the control of father or husband nor by domestic concerns: Pelagia, for instance, had a household of servants at her disposal. They presumed to send letters to bishops, and they come across in the stories as lively, intelligent women who had some knowledge of scripture.

The move from a life of pleasure to the hardships of the desert was in several cases preceded by a visit from one of the monks, who trusted himself to enter the presence of the beautiful but sinful women without being tempted. Reminded of the sharp and eternal torture that awaited them if they persisted in their way of life, the prostitutes were moved to burn or sell their belongings and follow the monk into the desert. Ward writes, "Unable to trust their own ideas and reactions, they take the sensible course of placing themselves in the hands of those who have revealed this truth to them, and at once each follows the opportunity for freedom that is so unexpectedly offered."[7] The freedom of desert life, however, was in vivid contrast to the freedom they had enjoyed formerly. Like their mentors, the "harlots of the desert" deprived themselves of food, wore hairshirts, and lived in narrow caves. One of them, Thais, at her own request, was sealed into a cell, dark, small, and filthy, and remained there alone for three years.

The women in the desert frequently dressed in the tunic and breeches of the men. This can be explained, of course, by the practical need to protect themselves. Ward suggests that, beyond that, there was an effort by both men and women in the desert to transcend gender. She claims that women's care not to present themselves in any way as a female was not a rejection of their femininity, but rather an assertion of it.[8] It seems more likely that the attempt to be seen as male was a result of the low esteem, not to say contempt, in which women were held by society at large and by the monks in particular. Amma Sarah's assertion, "According to my nature I am a woman but not according to my thoughts," suggests that women, when proven capable of thought and of reaching a high degree of spiritual development, are no longer women. She is reported as having said to visiting monks, "It is I who am a man, you who are women."[9] She is here not so much declaring her equality with men as she is subscribing to the commonly held notion that men were superior, and that to enter seriously onto a spiritual path was to become a man.

There is little to indicate, then, that the "harlots of the desert," once converted, significantly influenced the spirituality of the monks who preceded them there. They adopted unquestioningly and with enthusiasm the extreme asceticism that was the desert ideal. They gave up their wealth, comfort and pleasure, and repented of their former lives with a thoroughness that won them the admiration of all. Their function in the stories seemed to be to serve as examples of the essence of repentance, to demonstrate the extent of God's mercy which reaches even to harlots, and to edify the monks and all of the faithful who found to their astonishment that weak and wicked women could sustain as much and more than men in their search for forgiveness and for God.

Thomas à Kempis and the Imitation of Christ

The spirituality of the Eastern abbas and ammas was to affect Western Christian thought and practice for centuries. We hear echoes of it in the 15th-century spiritual classic *The Imitation of Christ.* Written in the Netherlands between 1420 and 1427, the book was translated into many European languages. Some 2,000 editions have appeared in English alone. Although the authorship of the book has been disputed, most scholars now accept Thomas à Kempis as the author. Thomas was born in Kempen, a town on the Rhine, north of Cologne. He was educated by the Brothers of the Common Life, and joined their association of clerics and lay people.[10] He became a monk of Mount St. Agnes in the diocese of Utrecht, and spent most of his life within the monastery walls.

Up until the Second Vatican Council, *The Imitation of Christ* was to be found on the bookshelves of virtually every novitiate, but its exhortations were not confined to religious. Thoughtful people of every age and vocation have found spiritual nourishment in the little volume. It was found on the shelves of George Eliot and Dag Hammerskjold, and was the book Pope John Paul I was reading on the night of his death.

That *The Imitation of Christ* has had its critics, as well as its devotees, is evident from a letter of William Thackeray written to Mrs. William Brookfield on Christmas Day, 1849. He writes:

> The scheme of that book carried out would make the world the most wretched useless dreary doting place of sojourn. . . . a set of selfish beings crawling about

avoiding one another, and howling a perpetual mise-
rere. . . . We know that deductions like this have been
drawn from the teachings of J.C.: but Please God the
world is preparing to throw them over.[11]

This description gives no hint of the touching passages
on peace and simplicity, spiritual rapture, resting in God,
the sweetness of Jesus, and the pleasures of a devout life.
Thackeray's comment is, in fact, a literary caricature. But
that said, it is true that Thomas' views on the flesh, the
world and social intercourse are quite as depressing as those
of his 3rd-century forebears. Self-knowledge leads to seeing
oneself as mean and abject, indeed, as a despicable worm.
The ordinary rounds of life: eating, drinking, sleeping, wak-
ing, resting, laboring – all are seen as misery and affliction
to the devout soul. "Woe to those who do not know their
own misery," writes Thomas, "and woe to those who love
this wretched and corruptible life."[12]

It is evident that the same dualities that mark the thought
of the Greek philosophers, the Fathers of the Church, and
the desert monks, are alive and well in *The Imitation of
Christ*. Thomas à Kempis opposes his human sensibility and
sensuality to reason, and associates the former with the law
of sin. The matter of our corruptible bodies, he tells us, is
the source of our inordinate concupiscence and of the
temptations which plague us. If we would conquer them,
we must crucify our "old nature," and do battle against the
flesh. This is the price the soul must pay if it is to rest in
God.

Ignatian Spirituality

As we move into the 16th century, we find in Ignatius of
Loyola a saint and spiritual director whose life, thought and
writings have had a profound influence on the development
of theology, ethics and spirituality in the Western world.

The story of his conversion is familiar to most: an ambitious and pleasure-loving soldier in the Spanish army until the age of 26, Ignatius turned to God and God's service after suffering an injury in the defense of the fortress of Pampeluna. The reading of a *Life of Jesus Christ* and lives of the saints during his convalescence proved to be the starting point of a journey that would lead him to mystical union with God and to the founding of the Society of Jesus.

Carefully analyzing his own religious experience, Ignatius Loyola developed a series of *Spiritual Exercises* designed to provide a method to lead souls to God. Elaborately systematized with preparatory prayers, preludes, reflections and dialogues, the exercises were at first meant to help young men discern their vocation, but they were adapted later to more general purposes and to the changing needs of Christians in every age.

Perhaps the most original contribution of Ignatius is the way in which he engages the spiritual seeker to call on memory, intellect, will, imagination and the five senses in the pursuit of holiness. This suggests a certain integration in Ignatius' approach to the interior life, and it witnesses to his psychological acumen. His approach is humane and flexible; he does not expect a slavish application of the method he sets out. Unlike some of the ascetics who preceded him, he is capable of encouraging us to enjoy ". . . appropriate pleasures of body and soul which may help [us] share in the gladness of [our] Creator and Redeemer."[13]

Ignatius Loyola was, nevertheless, influenced by Thomas à Kempis, and we find in the *Spiritual Exercises* the same tendencies toward deprivation, humiliation and abnegation that marked the monk of Mount St. Agnes. These are considered fit means to prepare one for prayer, for the performance of good works, and for attaining love for God through Christ. The Second Exercise is aimed at personal renewal. The third point of it reads:

Finally let me face the fact that my body is so entirely subject to infection, corruption, and repulsive disfigurement and that I myself am, as a person, a kind of spiritual cancer or abscess from the point of view that I have been the source of so many sins and other contagious evils.[14]

The body and self are once again things to be overcome and conquered.

Speaking of the spiritual quest as one of struggle and battle was fairly commonplace in the writings of the Desert Fathers and those of medieval authors. Ignatius Loyola, however, was to bring the metaphor to new heights; he had been, after all, an army officer. Jesus is presented to us as a head of state, a commander-in-chief whose flag we must prefer to the standard of the enemy camp, that is, Lucifer's. We are called to do spiritual combat in the service of our Master, King and Lord. Indeed, members of the new Society were characterized as those who "fight under the standard of the Cross" in the charter granted by Pope Paul III.

Ignatius never founded a female branch of the Society, but many congregations of women were profoundly influenced by Ignatian spirituality, however ill-suited its military metaphors were to their mentality. In some of these congregations, Ignatian principles were badly applied. Perhaps their Jesuit mentors did not trust them with the discretion allowed by Ignatius to his men. In any case, Sr. Jeanne-Françoise de Jaeger points out that the "discreet charity" which was to guide Jesuits in their prayer, meditation, study and penances, and which allowed them a certain latitude, was practically a dead letter in women's congregations.[15] There is little doubt that women religious suffered when Ignatian texts were taken out of context and applied literally and unimaginatively by Jesuits who saw their relationship to women religious as that of parent to children. This attitude affected not only the personal spiritual development of women religious, but also their ministerial service. Further-more, the centralization that characterized Ignatius' govern-ment often became in their case "a structure of authority at the service of a blind obedience rather than . . . an effective means for an apostolic coordination."[16]

Women today, both lay and religious, with their broad-ened access to education, and with a new-found trust in their own insights and experience, are rereading scripture and spiritual classics, such as those we have briefly consid-ered here. They savor in these texts all that opens their mind, soul and heart to mystic joy and deeper union with God, loving service and a commitment to justice. They reject, however, what Sandra Schneiders has described as the "body-denying, overly methodical, highly verbal and intel-lectual, muscular, vertical, conquering method of the spiri-tual life."[17]

Women's Spiritual Journey

Women have become acutely sensitive to the androcentrism and, at times, the blatant misogyny that have pervaded men's scriptural interpretation and spiritual advice. In their con-temporary search for a spirituality suited to their own ex-perience of God, self and relationships, feminists have not been content, however, simply to critique men's scriptural interpretation and spiritual advice. Rather, they have redis-covered the interior landscape of women writers, saints and mystics who described their inward journey in new accents and fresh metaphors. Julian of Norwich is one of these.

Julian of Norwich: Medieval Mystic

Julian lived as an anchoress. That is, she was confined to a simple room, or perhaps a few rooms, attached to the parish church of St. Julian in Norwich. A window opened out into the church so she could follow church services, and another looked out onto the street. The citizens of Norwich and travelers who had heard of Julian's encounters with God could approach this window and dialogue with the mystic who was yet so humane and practical. They found in her an ascetic, certainly, but her asceticism was not that of the Desert Fathers and Mothers. She ate simply but adequately; she lived not quite alone, enjoying the services of a companion or maidservant, and probably a cat.[18] Contemporary women might well envy the privacy, quiet and freedom that allowed Julian to attend so single-mindedly to God and to the stirrings of her soul.

This 14th-century mystic achieved an integration of elements rare in spiritual writings of any age. Jean Leclercq, O.S.B., writes:

> With great facility she reconciles the human and the mystical, the body and the spirit, the ordinary and the extraordinary, affectivity and intelligence, feeling and reflection, culture and piety, knowledge and spirituality, learning and love . . . theology and psychology . . . poetry and rigor of thought, beauty and truth . . . magination and reason, fidelity to tradition and freedom in its interpretation, unity of prayer and its varieties . . . and, finally, the human and the divine.[19]

Julian's literary style, as compared to the Scholastic theologians who proceeded by way of philosophical argument, is that of a charming, but far from facile, narrative. Her language is often that of courtly love; it abounds in earthy, colorful, touching images and metaphors. One of the most striking metaphors is that of God and Christ as Mother. She envisions the Trinity as Father, Mother, and Holy Spirit and writes: "In the first we have our being, and in the second we have our increasing, and in the third we have our fulfillment. The first is nature, the second is mercy, and the third is grace."[20]

God's motherliness comes through even when Julian uses the pronoun "he," as when she describes God as good and comforting, ". . . our clothing who wraps and enfolds us for love, embraces and shelters us, surrounds us for his love, which is so tender that he may never desert us."[21]

Just as Julian speaks of God as great, good and merciful, she presents the creatures whom God loves as noble and rich, pleasing to God as they achieve his will and glory. We may sin, out of ignorance and naivete, but sin has no ultimate reality.[22] It serves to sharpen our self-knowledge and deepen our sense of God's mercy. This, in turn, motivates us to amend our lives, and so we open ourselves yet more generously to God.

It is tempting here to reproduce the countless passages that open the eyes of one's soul to an inexpressibly wise, true, fair, sweet and forgiving God – a God who gazes fondly on those She has created and united in love to Her own being. It must suffice, instead, to recommend the entire text of her theologically sound and poetically lyrical reve-lations to all who wish to explore new dimensions of divine beauty.

Sor Juana Inés de la Cruz: Poet and Scholar

If we move forward to the 17th century and to New Spain, we find in Sor (Sister) Juana Inés de la Cruz another fore-mother who remained in oblivion for centuries, but who has recently come to light as a woman of extraordinary talent: a poet, playwright, theologian, musician, and painter. If Julian was first and foremost a mystic, Sor Juana was above all an intellectual. Her vehement, passionate desire for knowledge was the driving force of her life, and she caught on at a very tender age that her gender would be an obstacle in her search for it. She learned to read at the age of three or four, and by the time she was seven, begged her mother to dress her as a boy so that one day she could enter the University. That ambition was to be thwarted, but the young Inés Ramirez de Asbaje did get enough private lessons in Latin to serve as the basis for the classical education she gave herself.

At age 13, Inés was introduced to the court, where she became lady-in-waiting to the Marchioness of Mancera, whose husband was Viceroy of Mexico from 1664-1673. Inés's beauty and intelligence, vivacity, learning and wit compensated for what she lacked in status and wealth: she soon became the center of court culture and society. With no prospects for the kind of marriage that might possibly have provided the environment she needed for study, and feeling, in any case, a total antipathy for marriage, Inés entered a discalced Carmelite convent in 1667, at the age of 15. At this point, two volumes of her poetry had already been published in Spain. Finding the Carmelite discipline severe in the extreme, she left after three months and joined the Convent of Saint Paula of the Hieronymite Order in Mexico City. Here the young woman, already recognized as the most learned woman in Mexico, would find sufficient time, calm and space to devote herself to her intellectual interests.

Sor Juana's devotional writings contain none of the acts of penance, purification or self-inflicted pain that characterize other nuns' writings of 17th-century New Spain. Neither were they marked by the expressions of self-abasement and renunciation of will, mind and judgment common in these writings. On the contrary, she defends " . . . her right to learn, to judge, and to think for herself."[23] This right, as well as her right to give public voice to her literary gifts, was constantly being challenged by Sor Juana's enemies and friends alike. She was acutely aware that what would be considered merit in a man was, in her case, considered an anomaly, if not a downright perversion.

In several works, Sor Juana defends women's right to education and their right to participate in the intellectual order usually reserved to men. She insisted that the soul and mind were without gender. In a song in honor of St. Catherine of Alexandria, for instance, in which Sor Juana celebrates the saint's triumph over the philosophers, she writes:

> There in Egypt, all the sages
> by a woman were convinced
> that gender is not of the essence
> in matters of intelligence. Victor! Victor![24]

In another essay, a response to the Bishop of Puebla, who had advised her publicly to abandon secular letters, hinting that her soul would be in danger if she should not heed his counsel, Sor Juana respectfully defends her intellectual vocation and, coincidentally, that of all women who shared her passion for study. She furthermore defends the right of women to comment on and interpret scripture, if only privately.[25] Sor Juana did not make tidy divisions among the fields of knowledge; she saw in all of them a path to God. Nor did she make a sharp distinction between the Christian and the human. The whole realm of life and knowledge was a source of wisdom, capable of leading her to the brink of the infinite and into God's embrace.

In several works Sor Juana demonstrates her familiarity with the lives and works of women who excelled in sacred and secular studies: poets, prophets, philosophers and judges. In sonnets and elsewhere she celebrates learned women, both historical and mythical. She was obsessed, observes Octavio Paz, by the place of women in the world of the mind.[26] She refers to Mary, the Mother of God, as "The Supreme Doctor of the Divine Schools," and finds in the goddess Isis the archetype of highest learning, the universal Mother who represents earth and nature.

George Tavard, S.J., does not hesitate to call Sor Juana a theologian.[27] She was, he says, the first to choose beauty as the chief attribute of God, others having found God to be preeminently one, good or true. In terms of theological development, she stands between the scholastics who stressed analysis and modern theologians whose concern is wholeness.

In Sor Juana's vision, beauty and grace are related, and they are identical with love. Love finds its source in beauty; Christ sought human nature precisely because he was enamored of its beauty. Nature, God's first work, is born of God's creative love and is a fertile Mother who orders all things in harmony. Her elements are joined in inseparable links and form "a perfect circle, or mysterious chain."[28]

Far from mistrusting or despising the body, Sor Juana finds in bodily beauty a reflection of spiritual beauty. She sings of the beauty of her friend, the Countess of Pareda:

> Your body, caliper-wrought
> from proportion to persistence
> creates a divine harmony . . . [29]

The first theologian and feminist of colonial Mexico was to renounce study and writing in 1693, two years before her death. Paz offers a nuanced analysis of the possible reasons behind this decision, reasons ranging from historical circumstances, personal tensions, dictates of faith and conscience, and psychological need. Whatever the reasons, Sor Juana sold her 4,000-volume library and her musical and scientific instruments, and lived as a penitent. The part played by her confessor, the renowned Jesuit Nuñez de Miranda, and by the Bishop of Puebla were central in her abjuration of writing and the intellectual life. It is difficult to forgive them.

Sor Juana died of a disease contracted while ministering to her sisters, victims of the plague that raged through the

city. The last word has not been spoken about this remarkable woman, victim of her own gifts and of the absurd
misogyny and oppressive structures of her day.

Dorothy Day: Political Activist

In our own times, Dorothy Day exemplifies another aspect
of women's spirituality. She was a prophet and peacemaker,
who wrote and labored for more than six decades to build
a new and more just social order.

Born in Brooklyn on November 8, 1897, Day lived as
a child in Berkeley and Oakland, California, and in Chicago,
where her father earned a modest living as a sports and
fiction writer. Day attended the University of Illinois for two
years, and there developed both her taste for American
radicalism and her sensitivity to the poor. When her family
moved to New York, she followed them there and found
employment writing for socialist papers. Her companions
were the leftist intellectuals of Greenwich Village. Not content to simply talk and theorize, Day translated her political
convictions into social action, protesting the draft when the
United States entered into World War I, and picketing the
White House in the struggle for women's suffrage. It was
during her 30-day prison sentence for her participation in
this protest that Day read the Bible with attention. It was
the only book allowed the prisoners, and Day sought in it
some comfort in the midst of the isolation and desolation
she suffered.

In the years before her conversion to Catholicism, Day
had several romantic attachments. One involved her with a
newsman. This affair ended when Day, after agonizing debate
with herself, had an abortion. Next she entered into an
unhappy and short-lived marriage, and then into a
common-law marriage. The latter was a happy union with
Forster Batterham, and resulted in the birth of Day's daughter
and only child, Tamar Teresa. More and more drawn to prayer

and to Catholicism, Day decided to have her daughter baptized. Shortly afterward, Day herself was baptized into the Catholic Church. It was clear to her that this would spell an end to her relationship with Batterham, who was devoid of any religious belief or feeling. He looked upon her ". . . yearnings toward the life of the spirit . . ." as morbid escapism.[30] The separation was painful.

It was in 1932 that Dorothy Day met Peter Maurin, the French peasant and radical philosopher whose ideas would ignite Day and provide the framework for her lifework. Together they established and published the *Catholic Worker* and began the Catholic Worker houses of hospitality to feed and shelter the poor. Day herself would live in a Catholic Worker House, sharing the life of the destitute women and men she served and from whom, she insisted, she received as much as she gave. These were the people, the ". . . criminal, the unbalanced, the drunken, the degraded . . . " whom she would describe as her spiritual kin, the ones in whom she found Christ.[31]

Day's spirituality was an intriguing combination of traditional Catholic practice, prophetic vision, social activism and service to the poor. She adopted and advocated voluntary poverty, finding that the renunciation of material comfort and acquisitiveness opened up a wide path to freedom. She never confused voluntary poverty with the destitution suffered by the guests at her hospitality houses, however, and she never ceased to fight against the social structures, greed, and human indifference that caused and perpetuated such privation.

What strikes one about Day's interaction with the poor is the warmth and personal nature of it. She provided a true community for them, the kind of community St. Paul had in mind when he wrote to the churches, urging them to compassion, unity, mutual respect and loving care for one another. On one occasion, when a social worker wanted to know how long she let people stay in the Catholic Worker houses, she answered:

> . . . since there are no jobs, we let them stay forever. They live with us, they die with us and we give them a Christian burial. We pray for them after they are dead. Once they are taken in, they become members of the family. Or rather they were always members of our family. They are our brothers and sisters in Christ.[32]

Day's steadfast commitment to peace was an essential component of both her spiritual life and her political agenda. War was the antithesis of the Sermon on the Mount and of the works of mercy, both of which Day took seriously to heart. She protested publicly and vehemently against both World Wars and against the war in Vietnam. She wrote and spoke, participated in vigils, marches, and boycotts; she opposed the draft; she was imprisoned and she was reviled – all in the name of peace. Day was convinced that the conditions for a just war simply could not be met. It is interesting in our own day to see the Church inch toward her position.

Dorothy Day's spiritual quest was marked first and foremost by her hunger and thirst for justice, her commitment to the cause of peace, and her steady and energetic carrying out of the works of mercy. But beneath all of the activity, and sustaining it, was a capacity for contemplation and for delight and wonder in God's creation. She was in awe at the beauty and grace to be found in literature and, in equal or greater measure, in a mother holding and talking with her baby on a bus.[33] She savored the moments of silence, study, meditation and prayer that she managed to carve out for herself against all odds. Robert Coles quotes her as saying, "I think I talk in my sleep to God and the saints . . . I *know* I talk to them when I'm awake all the time." And she continued, "I hope what I'm saying makes me not quite a 'case,' not a fanatic, only some aging lady who is religiously obsessed.[34]

Obsessed, perhaps; certainly ablaze with love for God and neighbor, especially the working and the destitute poor. She would have none of being called a "saint," though. "That's the way people try to dismiss you," she said.[35]

Feminists find in Day both an ally and a critic. June E. O'Connor, professor of religious studies at the University of California-Riverside, points to some of the seeming contradictions in Day's views about women and women's roles.[36] She marched with the suffragists, and yet disdained the vote, feeling that the women most likely to use it were those who blindly supported a materialistic, violent and unjust American system. She found the suffragist movement and the subsequent women's liberation movement too middle-class and too self-centered; her basic sympathy was with the women of the ghettos and slums. She seemed to accept the conventional roles assigned to men and women, and held traditional views about marriage, but she herself was a single mother, often absent from her daughter because of her work and her political activities.

O'Connor points out that, although not a feminist in any self-conscious way and sometimes an outspoken critic of certain feminist stances, Day's views, actions, choices and commitments reveal a woman who had much in common with feminist thought and causes. She was conscious of inequities between the sexes, and felt that a greater balance was needed and was possible. She valued women's ability to see the whole, to integrate seemingly conflicting aspects of the human condition, to think with their whole bodies. She used her own experience as a starting point for her thought, writing and life choices. And she saw the links that connected social problems and injustices. O'Connor notes:

> . . . [Day] remarked, for example that the place of sex was as pertinent to questions of social justice as were

discussions of war, overpopulation, capital punishment, birth control, abortion, euthanasia, and the role of the state. She saw all of these issues as issues of power and control . . . [37]

Dorothy Day's spiritual depth and her religious faith were not separate from her sexuality. Indeed, all three were intimately connected. She considered her capacity to love, her pregnancy, her giving birth as so many paths to God; they made of her a co-creator with God, and they drew her closer to the source of all life.

Even this brief profile hints at the extraordinary cohesion of Dorothy Day's life: her ideas, convictions, feelings, actions, writings, spiritual insights and life choices illumined and strengthened one another. She found in the communal struggle the face of God, and realized that spiritual and social quests are ultimately one. Each served to deepen her understanding of and thirst for a world of genuine love, peace, freedom and reciprocity. She lived simply, nonviolently, prayerfully and justly; she knew intimately how exhausting the works of mercy can be. Dorothy Day's life and writings have added to the color and texture of women's spirituality.

The Contemporary Scene

Feminist spirituality today draws on the insights of women's spiritual heritage and on the many-faceted contemporary feminist movement. Its adherents include women who have returned to Goddess worship, women who practice witchcraft or Wicca, those who worship within mainstream denominations, and those who do not affiliate with any organized religion. Joined with voices from these quarters are those of women of every race and nation. They are speaking in new and powerful idioms of women's experience in a variety of cultures. Black, Hispanic and Asian women particularly are broadening and enriching the field of women's theology and spirituality through their analysis not only of patriarchal structures, but also of stubborn racial ones that have resulted in a triple oppression – race, gender, and class – of Third World and minority women. They challenge white women to examine their collusion in racism and to confront the ethics of using white power to gain privileges that benefit white women. Women of color, however, go beyond exposing the evils and the burden of the economic, sexual and emotional abuse of their sisters. Black, Hispanic and Asian scholars, among others, are examining the particular beauty and strength of their own spiritual heritage. Audre Lorde, African-American novelist, essayist and poet, highlights, for instance, the dynamic integration of spirituality, sensuality and politics in the spiritual vision of Black women. And Toinette Eugene, theologian, describes Black Christian spirituality as an ". . . embodied, incarnational, holistic and earthly reality and gift given to us by the God who became enfleshed to dwell with us as a 'body-person.'"[38]

Ivone Gebara, a Brazilian theologian, offers a new anthropology, one which substitutes the feminist values of reconciliation, interdependence and relationship for outworn patriarchal ones of individualism, isolation and competition.[39] And Chung Hyun Kyung, a Korean liberationist theologian, gives voice to the experience and struggles of Asian women. She describes their emerging spirituality as concrete, creative, prophetic, community-oriented, pro-life (in a manner, however, supportive of women's reproductive rights), ecumenical and creation-centered.[40]

The distinct voices of women of various cultures constitute the single-most significant and exciting development in feminist work in religion during the past 15 years.[41] They are transforming the field. Together with the pioneers in feminist theology and spirituality, minority women in the United States and women from around the globe are affecting the entire theological enterprise. In dialogue with one another, they draw on one another's scholarship, enrich one another's thought, and move one another toward greater clarity.

Whatever their differences, women drawn to feminist spirituality have many things in common. They are disillusioned with stubborn, prescribed sex roles which have, among other things, marginalized women and excluded them from significant activities within their churches. They are intent on finding a religious home for women, and freeing women from the strictures of a rigid, angry, punishing, male God; they are expanding symbols and metaphors for God in ways that enhance our understanding of divine being. They are leaving behind religious experience that is stiff, somber, culturally impoverished, and devoid of feeling, and embracing a spirituality that is joyous, hospitable and healthy. Feminist God-seekers are, furthermore, committed without apology to the empowerment of women, believing that women, fully empowered, will be effective agents in the creation of new social and cultural paradigms. They are exquisitely sensitive to the web that connects all parts of creation: humanity in its diversity, animals and every living being in their unique mystery, the entire universe in all of its beauty.

The Statement of Philosophy that appears in every issue of the journal *Woman of Power* neatly summarizes these ideas. It reads:

Woman's spirituality is a world-wide awakening of womanpower whose vision is the transformation of our selves and our societies.

The ancient spiritual voice of woman now speaks its long-hidden wisdom and becomes an active force for the conscious evolution of our world.

This emerging voice speaks of . . .

- *the recognition of the interconnectedness of all life*
- *the awareness that everything has consciousness and is sacred*
- *the re-membering of our selves as sacred beings, and the loving of our psyches, bodies and emotions*
- *the empowerment of women and all oppressed peoples*

- *the activation of spiritual and psychic powers*
- *the honoring of woman's divinity*
- *reverence for the earth, and the celebration of her seasons and cycles, and those of our lives.*

One of the most persistent themes in the thought and literature of women's spirituality is the need for integration and wholeness as an antidote to the harmful dualism that has marked Western philosophy, theology and spirituality since Greek antiquity. Feminist scholars have explored and exposed the stultifying consequences of splitting the universe into warring factions with heaven, men, mind, soul, spirit, speech, work and fruitful action on one side, and earth, women, body, feeling, silence and languorous passivity on the other. The war pits clearly unequal forces against one another: men on the side of heaven are destined to win control over all that is beneath them. Women with aspirations of entering the realm of thought and spirit are expected to wage similar battles over their unruly lower selves.

Feminist spirituality envisions the spiritual quest in quite other terms. Its theorists and practitioners call not for spiritual war, but for spiritual integration and wholeness. They celebrate rather than despise their own femaleness, the earth, body, feeling and imagination, even as they exercise their right to name God and to speak of soul, mind and spirit. They call for a world in which every dimension of human nature, every human faculty, every person, and every unique element of God's creation is considered sacred and held in reverence. They long to heal the inequalities, separations, and divisions that have robbed both men and women, but especially women, of the fullest expression of their being.

Feminist spirituality tends to see the male(spirit)/female (body) split as the foundational one.[42] Women engaged in a feminist, spiritual quest are intent on associating female and spirit while, at the same time, reinterpreting the female/body association and, ultimately, healing the spirit/body division. This has required a colossal effort. It has meant, to begin with, turning close attention to our bodies, listening to them, reverencing them, and celebrating them. It has involved liberating ourselves from the dictates of a society that invites us to do battle with our own bodies in order to get them to conform to society's norms of the female body-beautiful: willowy, if not emaciated, fit, firm, young and flawless. That image is in stark contrast to real women's bodies, which come in an admirable variety of sizes, shapes and colors. It is in painful contrast to the bruised bodies of women who have been the subjects of rape, incest, and battering. Liberating our bodies has meant liberating ourselves from the effects of this treatment, and from the internalizing of the shame, guilt, rage and resentment connected with it. It has meant gazing on ourselves with self-accepting eyes, and on each other with loving wonder as we celebrate the contours of every woman's body and the way in which each graces the world

When the healing of body and spirit begins, women see with awe-ful clarity the exquisite links that join these two. We realize that we are spirit in physical form, and we begin to enjoy a sense of ease and pleasure in our own embodiedness. We discover in our bodies a major source of wisdom and power; we appreciate anew what we always instinctually felt, namely, that our bodies are the sacred means of connecting us to God, nature, loved ones and the human community. We become whole, and bring our wholeness to the creative work of fashioning a just and violence-free world.

Endnotes

1. Anne Carr, "On Feminist Spirituality," in *Women's Spirituality: Resources for Christian Development,* ed. Joann Wolski Conn (New York: Paulist Press, 1986), 49.
2. Benedicta Ward, SLG, *The Sayings of the Desert Fathers* (Kalamazoo: Cistercian Publications, 1975), 151.
3. *Ibid.,* 35.
4. *Ibid.,* 43.
5. Cf. Mary Daly, *Pure Lust, Elemental Feminist Philosophy* (Boston: Beacon Press, 1984), 36-37.
6. See Benedicta Ward, SLG, *Harlots of the Desert* (Kalamazoo: Cistercian Publications, 1987).
7. *Ibid.,* 80
8. *Ibid.,* 63.
9. *Ibid.*
10. See *The Imitation of Christ by Thomas à Kempis,* trans. E.M. Dlaiklock (Nashville: Thomas Nelson Publishers, 1979), 8.
11. Quoted in William Creasy, *The Imitation of Christ by Thomas à Kempis, A New Reading of the 1441 Latin Autograph Manuscript* (Macon, Ga.: Mercer University Press, 1989), xvi.
12. Harold C. Gardiner, S.J., *The Imitation of Christ, Thomas à Kempis, A modern version based on the English translation made by Richard Whitford around the year 1530* (Garden City, New York: Doubleday, 1955), 61.
13. Lewis Delmage, S.J., *Spiritual Exercises of St. Ignatius Loyola* (New York: Joseph F. Wagner, Inc., 1968), 113.
14. *Ibid.,* 34.
15. See "Women's Congregations that Follow an Ignatian Spirituality: A Report by Sr. Jeanne-Françoise de Jaeger" in *Ignatian Spirituality Since CG 32* (Rome, Italy: Centrum Ignatianum Spiritualitatis, n.d.), 91.

16. *Ibid.*
17. "Women's Experience and Spirituality," *Spirituality Today* (Summer 1983): 109.
18. See Carol Lee Flinders, *Enduring Grace, Living Portraits of Seven Women Mystics* (San Francisco: Harper, 1993), 81.
19. *Julian of Norwich, Showings,* trans. Edmund Colledge, OSA and James Walsh, S.J. (New York: Paulist Press, 1978), 13.
20. *Ibid.,* 294.
21. *Ibid.,* 183.
22. Flinders, 90.
23. Asuncion Lavrin, "Unlike Sor Juana? The Model Nun in the Religious Literature of Colonial Mexico," in *Feminist Perspectives on Sor Juana Inés de la Cruz,* ed. Stephanie Merrim (Detroit: Wayne State University Press 1991), 79.
24. Quoted in Octavio Paz, *Sor Juana or the Traps of Faith,* trans. Margaret Sayers Peden, (Cambridge: Harvard University Press, 1988), 435.
25. See *The Answer/La Respuesta,* edited and translated by Electa Arenal and Amanda Powell (New York: The Feminist Press at the City University of New York, 1994). This book presents the English translation together with the Spanish original, and provides an excellent Introduction which places the writing in its cultural setting of imperial New Spain.
26. *Ibid.,* 178.
27. See George Tavard, *Juana Inés de la Cruz and the Theology of Beauty: The First Mexican Theology* (Notre Dame: University of Notre Dame Press, 1991), ch. 7.
28. *Ibid.,* 204.
29. *Ibid.,* 192.
30. William D. Miller, *Dorothy Day* (San Francisco: Harper and Row, 1982), 188.
31. *Ibid.,* 343.
32. *Ibid.,* 283.
33. Cf. Robert Coles, *Dorothy Day, A Radical Devotion* (Reading, Mass.: Addison-Wesley Pub. Co., Inc., 1987), 158.
34. *Ibid.,* 143.
35. Quoted in William O. Paulsell, *Tough Minds, Tender Hearts, Six Prophets of Social Justice* (New York: Paulist Press, 1990), 85.
36. The Moral Vision of Dorothy Day, A Feminist Perspective (New York: Crossroad, 1991), ch. 2.
37. *Ibid.,* 41.
38. "Moral Values and Black Womanists," *Journal of Religious Thought* 44/2 (Winter-Spring 1988): 25.

39. See Ofelia Ortega, ed., *Women's Visions* (Geneva: WCC Publications, 1995), 71-72.

40. See *Struggle to Be Sun Again*, (Maryknoll, N.Y.: Orbis Books, 1990), 91-96.

41. The following works, in addition to those cited above, will give readers some idea of the scope and depth of this work: Linda A. Moody, *Women Encounter God: Theology Across the Boundaries of Difference* (Maryknoll, N.Y.: Orbis Books, 1996); Cheryl J. Sanders, ed., *Living the Intersection: Womanism and Afrocentrism in Theology,* (Minneapolis: Fortress Press, 1995); Delores Williams, *Sisters in the Wilderness: The Challenge of Womanist God-Talk* (Maryknoll, N. Y.: Orbis Books, 1993); Nancy Auer Falk and Rita M. Gross, *Unspoken Worlds: Women's Religious Lives,* (Belmont, Ca: Wadsworth Publishing Co., 1989); Ada Maria Isasi-Diaz and Yolanda Tarango, *Hispanic Women: Prophetic Voice in the Church* (San Francisco: Harper and Row, 1988); Letty Russell and others, *Inheriting Our Mothers' Gardens: Feminist Theology in Third World Perspective* (Philadelphia: Westminster Press, 1988); Renita J. Weems, *Just a Sister Away: A Womanist Vision of Women's Relationships in the Bible* (San Diego: Lura Media, 1988); Katie G. Cannon and others, *God's Fierce Whimsy* (New York: The Pilgrim Press, 1985); Audre Lorde, *Sister Outsider: Essays and Speeches,* (Trumansburg, New York: Crossing Press, 1984); Alice Walker, *In Search of Our Mothers' Gardens* (New York: Harcourt Brace, 1983).

42. Cf. Sandra Schneiders, *Beyond Patching: Faith and Feminism in the Catholic Church* (New York: Paulist Press, 1991), 75.

Chapter 2

Women and Ethics

Just as women's spirituality is transforming and enriching our concepts of the spiritual life, so are women's reflection and analysis changing the framework of traditional ethics. So profound are the questions raised that Margaret Farley wrote 20 years ago of the beginnings of a moral revolution.[1] Farley's rethinking of sin and evil and of what constitutes the common good was rooted in a new understanding of the "nature" of woman and the relation between the sexes. Spurred on by the women's movement, she and other feminist theologians reexamined and rejected the symbol of Eve as the embodiment of temptation and the source of evil, and the related notion of woman as weak-willed, inferior to man and, therefore, in need of his direction and control. They proposed that the patterns of dominance and subordination that had characterized the relations between the sexes be replaced by relations of equality and mutuality; and they found in the life of the trinity a basis and model for the kind of reciprocity that would lead both sexes to greater wholeness.

The incipient revolution did not stop at the level of personal relationships. The rethinking of ethical foundations called into question the morality and power dynamics of civil, social and ecclesiastical institutions as well. How did the question of dominant-subordinate relations play out in these arenas? Women began to refocus old questions and throw a spotlight on new ones in both the private and the public domains: Who defines goodness and evil, virtue and vice? What, from women's perspective, constitutes moral character? Do the traits valued in women keep them from acquiring social power? How does the concept of justice operate in the realm of family structures? What part does gender play in the areas of poverty and economic justice? How do an ethics of justice and rights relate to an ethics of care and responsibility? What kind of morality shapes our attitudes toward children, the ill, the aged, friends and lovers? It was a novelty to explore these questions from women's points of view because for centuries the field of morality had been a male preserve.

Women's exclusion from the human task of discerning what constitutes moral behavior, moral freedom and moral obligation was justified by the belief that women lacked a sense of justice, and for this reason were properly confined to the private and domestic worlds. Freud attributed women's deficient moral capacity to their sexuality, the predominance of envy in their mental life, and to their weak ability to sublimate their instincts. Worse still, Rousseau viewed women as essentially disordered, and held them responsible for engendering all the vices. Hegel was convinced that womankind constituted an enemy within the gates of a community, and that governments where women held power were in the gravest jeopardy.[2] Christian ethicists shared these views. Original Sin was Eve's fault, and her daughters proved to be emotional, intrusive, evil troublemakers whose frail ethical sense required their subordination to men, their intellectual and moral superiors.

Firmly in control of moral decision-making, men established systems that reflected their world view and reinforced existing power relationships. These systems assumed that in human relationships, someone (ideally, a white, proper-tied male) legitimately exercised power and control over those supposedly less well-endowed with reason and moral probity (e.g., females, blacks and colonials). These views constituted, obviously, a disparaging view of women and all others judged to be morally and intellectually inferior. Beyond that, by excluding women from ethical discourse, they rendered it a male rather than a fully human enterprise. Men's ethical judgment and standards masqueraded as universal, human norms, even though they failed to take into account women's historical experience, personal lives and moral outlook.

There were women through the centuries who questioned theories of women's nature that precluded their speaking with authority in the realms of theology, spirituality, and ethics. It wasn't until the 20th century, however, that women's access to the academy and their sustained feminist analysis permitted the emergence of alternate ways of constructing reality and, therefore, of envisaging human relationships and moral behavior.

One of the first voices to be heard was that of Valerie Saiving Goldstein. In an often-quoted article which appeared first in 1960, Saiving Goldstein critiqued Reinhold Niebuhr's *The Nature and Destiny of Man*, a series of lectures given in Scotland at the outbreak of World War II.[3] The historical moment undoubtedly influenced Niebuhr's broad-ranging and insightful analysis of the modern dilemma marked by *angst* pride, and the will-to-power. Niebuhr characterized pride as the basic human failing – pride which leads to the desire to be self-sufficient, to be free of entangling human relations, and to reign as a god who can subject others to one's will.

Saiving Goldstein noted that while Niebuhr's analysis of human nature and destiny reflected accurately many of the tendencies of men and nations, it failed to take into account women's experience precisely as women. Women did not stand to benefit from Niebuhr's exhortation to the practice of self-sacrificial love, however salutary the advice might be for self-absorbed and self-assertive men. Women's temptations are quite other than self-assurance and the will-to-power; they are, rather, the lack of an organizing center or focus, dependence on others for self-definition, underdevelopment, and the negation of self. Women's sin is not pride, but a tendency to self-effacement and a failure to attain full self-realization.

This critique of Niebuhr, a noted and gifted male ethicist-theologian, opened the way for a close look at traditional ethics, and for an articulation, increasingly rich and nuanced, of a feminine and a feminist ethics.

Feminine/Feminist Ethics

Feminist scholars distinguish between these two approaches to ethics, and between them and "women's ethics."[4] Feminine and feminist moral perspectives are as relevant to men as to women, and they are interrelated, although each has a distinctive emphasis.

A feminine approach to ethics gives expression to women's unique voice. It rises from a feminine consciousness which emphasizes and values the gender traits traditionally associated with women: listening, nurturing, tending to relationships, socializing young children, caring for the old. These are the "virtues" exercised in the private realm. The fact that women, rather than typical men, tend to develop them is attributed variously to biological, psychological and socioeconomic factors. Critics of this approach point out that it flirts with suggesting that character traits are determined by gender. They fear that a certain reading of works in this vein could imprison women and men in traditional roles, giving women an unwanted monopoly on the admittedly attractive and socially necessary traits of caring, nurturance and compassion, and trapping men in roles that cut them off from these humanizing tendencies.

A feminist approach to ethics, on the other hand, is political in the sense that it recognizes and deplores women's continued subordination and seeks to eliminate it. It is rooted in ". . . women's growing awareness of the disparity between received traditional interpretations of their identity and function and their own experience of themselves and their lives."[5] This new awareness and the ethics that flow from it can be couched in the vocabulary and founded on the principles of various political traditions: liberal, socialist, Marxist, radical.

Feminist ethics looks with suspicion on the kind of disembodied rationality that has been the hallmark of traditional ethics, and prefers instead to combine reason with history, myth, revelation, intuition, feeling and imagination in its attempts to reconstruct the tradition. The resulting ethical norms, respecting as they do the historical and cultural context of individuals and groups, avoid the kind of abstract universals or rigid absolutes that have characterized traditional ethics.

Central to feminist ethics are the notions of relationship and community. These values are juxtaposed to the isolation and individualism that are presumed by many ethicists working in the Western European tradition to be the most salient features of the human condition. Feminine ethics refers to personal relations more readily, perhaps, than does feminist ethics, but both speak the language of relationship more readily than the language of principles, rules, and rights. Feminists, in their search for just and satisfying relationships, insist both on women's need for autonomy and self-determination, and on mutuality as a necessary ingredient in human relations. They understand persons to be ". . . embodied subjects, with an essential capacity and need for union with other persons."[6] They don't, however, romanticize relationships or human attachments, and they reject outright theories of the complementarity of the sexes which cast women in the role of servant and deprive them of freedom, personal identity and individual worth. Furthermore, they acknowledge the particularity of all persons as an important consideration in determining what is morally right or wrong.

We can look upon feminine and feminist ethics, then, as a corrective to traditional ethics, which has generally been based on men's experience and has ignored or depreciated women's values. In claiming moral agency for themselves, women have turned attention to hitherto-neglected areas, ones of interest to them as women, and have re-interpreted ethical perspectives from their point of view. In doing so, they do not intend to deny or exclude the interests and values of men, nor do they claim the kind of absolute moral authority they decry in traditional systems. Rather they enter as equal partners into the dialogue about what constitutes authentic morality, convinced of the value of their own insights in addressing the moral dilemmas of our age. They bring to the exchange their own deeply felt needs and aspirations. Christian feminists bring to it the further conviction that the Gospel calls us both to individual moral freedom and to communal solidarity, to shared power rather than to coercive authority, and to reciprocity rather than to domination.

What ethical issues have feminists begun to explore? What have they contributed to the "feminization" of ethics? How have they expanded and enriched moral discourse? Without pretending that there is a single feminine or feminist voice, we can suggest some general lines of thought in areas that have attracted the attention, and often the passionate response, of women thinkers. One such area is that of the construction of ethics into separate domestic and public spheres.

Ethics in the Private and Public Arenas

The dualism that marks much of Western philosophical and political thought has not spared the realm of public versus personal, domestic, or private activity. This is particularly true since the advent of the industrial and capitalist state. We are only slowly and incompletely emerging from an ethic that assigns the world of business, finance, and government to men and the world of hearth and home to women. In this scenario, men do the world's real work, and return from the fray to the haven of their home to be renewed, refreshed and nourished by their self-sacrificing wives. The public sphere is the sphere of justice, the one in which, writes Seyla Benhabib, ". . . male heads of household transact with one another, while the domestic-intimate sphere is put beyond the pale of justice and restricted to the reproductive and affective needs of the bourgeois paterfamilias."[7] Thus, continues Benhabib:

> An entire domain of human activity, namely, nurture, reproduction, love and care, which become the woman's lot in the course of the development of modern, bourgeois society, is excluded from moral and political considerations, and relegated to the realm of nature.[8]

Reinhold Niebuhr, writing in 1965, concurred with the assignation of justice to the public realm and love to the private. Sacrificial love, he held, was:

> . . . a moral norm relevant to interpersonal (particularly family) relations, and significant for parents (particularly mothers, heroes and saints), but scarcely applicable to the power relations of modern industry.[9]

Self-sacrificial love could hardly be expected to operate in a world where competing groups properly worked as hard as possible to further their own interests. Here it was the role of justice to weigh, judge and balance conflicting interests and rights.

Feminists challenge this assignment of loving self-sacrifice to the home, the domain of women, and of energetic
assertiveness and the rational dispensation of justice to the
world of business and government. They see the division
as detrimental to both spheres. Women, already prone to
an unhealthy self-abnegation, have an obligation to themselves to weigh others' needs against their own, whether at
home or at work outside the home. Their self-realization
requires that they claim their own power and authority and
their right to well-being, and that they participate actively
in the creation of a humane culture in every area of life, a
task to be shared with men both in the workplace and at
home. Men, on the other hand, might give more serious
consideration to the call to serve, and the worlds of tech-
nology, business, finance and government would profit by
the cultivation of other-regard. The unrelenting pursuit of
profit has created victims, and has resulted in a kind of
alienation that touches both women and men, both home
and business.

Feminists, then, are engaged in bridging the gap that
dictates a different set of ethical principles to be applied in
the private and public realms. Assigning virtue to the home
and to women, while tolerating blatant immorality in the
marketplace, has ultimately disastrous effects. The division,
furthermore, is a spurious one. A familiar dictum of the
women's movement is that the personal is political. In reality,
the public and personal find their reality in the heart and
mind of each individual. Ideally, the actions and decisions
that flow from that source will have as their aim the flourishing of all persons affected by our actions and decisions.
Those who claim allegiance to a Christian ethic will be
particularly sensitive to the effect actions have on the un-
derprivileged, the economically deprived and the exploited.

Underlying the attempt to construct an ethical system
that integrates the private and public realms is a redefinition

of Christian love in terms of mutuality.[10] Niebuhr had ascribed mutual love to the non-religious realm, based as it is on the expectation of a return of the affection one gives. True Christian love (*agape*), he held, does not seek a return, although it is, paradoxically, the condition for complete mutuality. Anders Nygrens, too, as Barbara Hilkert Andolsen points out, asserts that *agape* is utterly self-sacrificing and self-forgetful; there is no room within it for self-love."[11] Feminists are suspicious of the concept of total self-sacrifice as being at the heart of Christian love, particularly when the notion is applied principally to women in the home. Margaret Farley speaks from a feminist stance when she describes Christian love as mutual love, a love exchanged between equals, both of whom are ready to give and take, possess and surrender, and both of whom are equally open, communicative and interdependent. This kind of love is applicable to both the domestic and civil spheres, where its growth and development depend on a roughly equal distribution of power, a point best understood by those whose power has been severely limited.

Christian love is but one of the virtues that women have reexamined, and pride but one of the vices they have explored from their point of view. The whole question of what constitutes good and evil calls for redefinition, and the whole panoply of virtues and vices deserves to be illumined from a feminist perspective.

Virtues and Vices Revisited

The renaming of good and evil has required a major recentering of the stories we tell of human corruption and salvation. Told by women's voices, we find that the stories reveal new emphases, new twists and turns, and that they hold out a promise of "justice for all." In their reexamination of virtues and vices, what have women had to say of obedience, anger and the functioning of justice?

Obedience

A morality of command and obedience has commonly marked male/female relationships, and has extended beyond them to embrace relations among classes, races and nations. This morality assigns command to the powerful elite and unquestioning obedience to the weak, poor, and powerless.

Some have seen obedience as the keystone of Christian ethics, envisaging God as the Supreme Ruler, the Almighty, before whom humanity, weak and powerless, bows in humble submission. For those who would be as gods, those who long for or who enjoy quasi-absolute political, economic or military power, God's sovereign power can serve as a kind of legitimation of their own. Sharon D. Welch speaks of the "erotics of domination" that permeates their thinking and their coercive authority.[12] By claiming willing acquiescence to a higher power, God, and by imagining themselves agents of God's will, they demand uncritical acceptance of their decrees. Being themselves slaves to the Lord, they can justify their brutal exercise of power over others. Elaine Pagels demonstrates that St. Augustine himself came to endorse total control, whether by the Church or by the State, finding in human weakness an excuse and a warrant for the exercise of undisputed power.[13]

Dorothy Sölle is among the Christian feminists who challenge the concept of human beings as powerless and as properly subject to superior powers, divine or human, who control our destiny and obstruct our self-determination. And she, together with increasing numbers of mainstream Catholic women, finds the image of God as Lord and Supreme Ruler not only wanting but injurious. "Why," she asks pointedly, "should we honor and love a being who does not transcend the moral level of contemporary culture as shaped by men, but instead establishes it?"[14] Women are seeking a God with whom they can be one, not to whom they must be subject. They are finding in God not a master who demands their self-denial, but a friend and companion who furthers rather than resents their growth, power and fulfillment.

The discovery by women, and by others who have been marginalized, of their own authority threatens the status quo, while obedience is a virtue that helps maintain it. But is the maintenance of the status quo what the Gospel calls us to? Are we not called, instead, to imagine new possibilities and to challenge laws and systems that impede them? Sölle, in *Creative Disobedience*, suggests that "phantasy" rather than obedience is at the center of the Christian ethical system. It is phantasy that enables us to envisage change and break through boundaries. It restores our spontaneity and sense of play; it unchains the powers that lie within us. Sölle speaks of the phantasy of Jesus, a gift that allowed him to ignore rules and prescriptions when they stood in the way of others' needs. His vision enabled him to see through and to level the categories that stratified and separated people. His ". . . soaring phantasy," writes Sölle, "really acknowledges but a single principle: the creation and the propagation of well-being."[15]

A feminist approach to ethics, then, reexamines the concept of obedience and of a Sovereign and All-Powerful Ruler who requires the passive submission of His subjects. God asks instead that we be co-creators in bringing to realization the vision that Jesus' phantasy enkindled when he walked among us.

Anger

St. Thomas Aquinas recognized that there were two ways of sinning through anger. One was to be angry without due cause; the other was not to be angry enough when the situation called for it. The conditioning of women makes it difficult for them to experience and express the righteous anger that the indignities, scorn and violence visited upon them merit. Good girls, after all, are compliant and are meant to swallow these things. Many profess astonishment that battered wives often blame themselves for their husbands' violence. This strange phenomenon, however, has its roots in women's undervaluation of themselves and in the self-censure that permits no anger-driven resistance.

While recognizing that a steady diet of angry indignation is neither healthy nor productive, women have come to appreciate the place of justified rage in changing systems that oppress them and others. The women of Greenham Commons, who for years have protested at the British missile site located there, sing:

> We are gentle, angry women
> And we are singing, singing for our lives.

Their song expresses the combination of love, compassion and anger that underlies the conviction and political action of women working for peace and justice. Beverly Wildung Harrison explores precisely this relationship in her essay "The Power of Anger in the Work of Love."[16] Anger, she insists, is not the opposite of love. On the contrary, it is a "vivid form of caring." It connects us, as does every emotion, with others, and it serves to signal that all is not well in a relationship. When anger is hidden or suppressed, our power to love is weakened; the possibility of deepening a relationship, or creating authentic community, is denied. Anger is a source of energy. It empowers us to act in order to change what we judge to be amiss, whether in our personal relations or in social and ecclesiastical institutions.

Women in the church are less and less fearful of giving voice to their anger. Those who are beyond anger are also beyond the hope of change, and have left the church. The anger of those who remain should be read as a positive sign. Angry women in the church have not abandoned hope that relations in the church can be reciprocal, that their voices can be heard, listened to and appreciated. There are some indications that women's love and anger, and the action that springs from both, are having some effect. The Jesuits at their 34th General Congregation, held in 1995, spoke to women in accents that women found refreshing. In their document entitled "Jesuits and the Situation of Women in Church and Civil Society," they acknowledge that they have been part of "a civil and ecclesial tradition that has offended against women," and that they were often reluctant in the past to admit there was a problem. They evince a real understanding of some of the issues women, and particularly feminists, have been underscoring for the past 30 years: systematic discrimination, violence against women, the feminization of poverty. They acknowledge with gratitude the contribution of women to their ministry and to reshaping their theological tradition. And they express a desire to move forward in solidarity with women to bring about a respectful reconciliation, a "more just relationship between women and men." This is a welcome response to women's anger, to women's call for change. Too often, the response of men in the church has been to ignore women's voices, blame the victims, or to insist that the real problem is not sexism but feminism.

Pope John Paul II, for instance, has consistently enraged women by his defensiveness or condescension, his failure to hear how women understand themselves, and his attempt to silence discussion on the ordination of women. The letter he addressed to women on the eve of the World Conference on Women, held in Beijing, however, gave hope that some light is breaking on the Vatican. Sound feminist insights inform large sections of the letter, and the Pope refers to the women's liberation movement as ". . . substantially a positive one, even if it is still unfinished, due to the many obstacles which, in various parts of the world, still prevent women from being acknowledged, respected, and appreciated." He presses for "an effective and intelligent campaign for the promotion of women," and he speaks of equal responsibility and reciprocal relations between men and women.[17] There is a note of conviction, warmth, and sincerity about the letter which women would be ungracious not to recognize. Indeed, they have welcomed the change of tone that marks much of the letter.

Nevertheless, John Paul II resorts once again to an outworn theological anthropology to discuss the relationship of men and women, and familiar, profoundly discouraging observations reveal a failure to understand or accept basic insights of respected scholars. Thus, "iconic complementarity" serves as a pretext for the continued exclusion of women from the sacramental priesthood; it is "by giving themselves to others each day [that] women fulfill their deepest vocation"; and women who proceed with pregnancies that are the result of rape win the praise and appreciation of the Pope. John Paul II's letter may temper the tide of unease and anger that is rising, not only in women but in many men as well, but his well-intentioned words will not actually stem it.

The fact is, where justice has not yet been attained, anger will have a role to play. While dealing with it is never a pleasant task, we can learn to recognize its place in the work of love and in the work of social transformation.

Justice

Some feminists, in their efforts to distinguish women's and men's approach to ethics, have suggested that while men focus on rights and duties, women focus on care, nurturance and relationship. "Difference feminism," as it is called, has a certain allure because it broadens understanding for what are considered female values and behaviors, and wins respect for them. On the other hand, difference feminism runs the risk of strengthening and perpetuating a system that identifies men with the principled application of justice in the "real" world and women with benevolent care in the home. It suggests that only men can speak the language of justice and only women can be sensitive to emotional context and personal need. And it sanctions men's sacrifice of intimacy for autonomy and women's sacrifice of autonomy for intimacy. Rosemarie Tong observes:

> Even if women are better carers than men (for whatever reasons), it may still be . . . ethically or politically unwise to associate women with the value of care. To link women with caring is to promote the view that women care by nature. It is also to promote the view that because women can and have cared, they should always care no matter the cost to themselves.[18]

Caring, under the conditions of a patriarchal system, can be distorted because forced by economic dependency, a psychological need to feed men's ego, or social pressure to enhance men's status. Authentic caring will be free, and will empower both giver and receiver.

We know from experience that both women and men are capable of speaking the language of justice *and* the language of care, and are, one hopes, becoming more capable of doing so. Men can learn to reciprocate the kind of care which they tend to take for granted, and women can learn to recognize when caring has ceased to be free and healthy and has become instead an instrument of their own victimization or disempowerment.

Women, in turning their attention to justice issues, have focused questions on issues that have by and large escaped the notice of men. Insisting on women's dignity and full humanity, they have protested discrimination in the workplace, in schools, in the courts and in the churches. They have examined the economic and social factors that keep women in low-paying jobs outside the home, without relieving them of major responsibility for the household and child care. They have sought control over their own bodies, especially in the area of reproductive rights, and they have brought to the full light of public attention the widespread practice of wife-beating. In short, women have examined structures and institutions from the viewpoint of their own experience, and have called for an end to whatever within these structures keeps women down and disadvantaged.

Underlying all of the issues that have been the subject of women's analysis and the object of their protest and strategic action is the imbalance of power in church and society, a basic justice issue. The concentration of power in the hands of Euro-American men, especially when that power is exercised in callous, coercive ways, is itself a moral problem, but one that has not received much attention in traditional ethics. Here the emphasis has been on the moral failings of the powerless rather than the deficiencies of the mighty. By examining rights, obligations and responsibilities from the perspective of those without power, women are shifting the center of familiar moral paradigms. By suggesting that sin on the part of the oppressed consists, not in resisting definitions imposed by others, but in accepting them, by emphasizing not the immorality of misusing freedom (an issue most relevant to the powerful) but the immorality of failing to claim the freedom God offers to all, women and others on the periphery are beginning to change the vocabulary of moral reflection.

As they do so, the links that connect the injustice suffered by women, the poor of the world, various ethnic and racial groups, gays, lesbians and the victims of war become increasingly clear. Some brands of justice are blind to the suffering that has diminished the lives of people in all of these groups. By focusing on the power imbalance that permits this suffering, oppressed groups are touching on an essential key to the transformation of unjust social structures.

Mary Daly's is the most original and radical voice raised in the discussion of what constitutes justice and injustice in the minds of the power brokers on the one hand, and in the minds of what she calls the "touchable class" on the other.[19] In patriarchal contexts, she claims, the words justice and injustice apply to "petty paternal disputes" which are either inimical or irrelevant to the aspirations of women (and by extension to other marginal groups). By naming for themselves what constitutes righteous virtues, by *creating* justice rather than simply struggling for it, by reinterpreting courage and prudence, temper and temperance, distemper and distemperance, anger and passion (which Daly herself does with rare wit and originality), women free themselves and begin to slake their hunger and thirst for creative "be-ing." Daly moves us to transcend the justice-injustice dichotomy, and to imagine new definitions, new concords, new worlds where the creative energy, not only of women but of all the historically oppressed, is let loose to effect a moral revolution of epic proportions.

Violence Against Women

In rethinking ethical frameworks, women have brought to the fore issues long neglected in reflection on moral behavior. Violence against women is one of them. The depth and breadth of the physical, psychological, and economic violence suffered by women has only recently surfaced as a breach of human rights. The sheer extent of violence against women, its commonplace-ness, has served paradoxically to render it semi-invisible. Furthermore, social, cultural and religious traditions have served to justify it. But tales of horror from around the world are beginning to break the wall of silence that has surrounded this issue. Feminist ethicists are asking why the law has proved better able to protect men against women's accusations than to protect women from men's assaults. Claudia Card invites women to consider:

> . . . how should women (and men) meet misogynist violence, much of which is socially sanctioned? how are we to recognize its forms, in others and in our ourselves? to shield ourselves, and heal ourselves, from its damage? to create environments in which we are not so totally shaped by it and by daily needs to do something about it? when, and how, are we justified in meeting violence with violence? what values help structure sane answers to such questions?[20]

As women ask these questions they begin to shed the guilt, fear, shame and powerlessness that have helped to hide and justify violence against them; they begin to create networks of solidarity and to expose the men who misuse them. They bring before the public eye the domestic rape, incest, battering and stalking that have haunted their lives.

Mary Daly was, again, one of the first to unveil in detail and from a feminist point of view the atrocities of Chinese footbinding, the practice of female genital mutilation in Africa, and the Indian custom of suttee by which women were expected to sacrifice themselves on a funeral pyre upon the deaths of their husbands.[21] Footbinding and suttee are now outlawed, but forced pregnancies (Romania), forced sterilization and abortion (China), and forced prostitution (Thailand and other Asian countries) are contemporary forms of violence against the bodily integrity of women. And rape, a universal phenomenon, is yet another.

In the United States a woman is raped every six minutes, more frequently even than a woman is beaten, which is every 18 minutes. In the early 80s in our country, there were about three-quarters of a million attempted or completed rapes. Rape often has racist and classist overtones: poor women and women of color are raped more often than white women. Jewish women suffered rape in pogroms, and black women were systematically raped in the ante-bellum South, victims of the economic subjugation of blacks by whites.

Rape during wartime is a commonplace – from biblical times right up to the recent Bosnian conflict, when Muslim women were the hapless victims of Serb soldiers. Mass rapes took place in France and Belgium during World War I; Pakistani soldiers raped more than 200,000 Bengali women during nine months of terror in the 1971 rebellion; American soldiers raped Vietnamese women in brutal, public, gang-rape scenes. Shiro Azuma, who served as an Imperial Army soldier in Japan, and who is now trying to air the truth about Japanese war deeds during World War II, said in an interview with the *Los Angeles Times*, "When we raped the women, we thought of them as humans, but when we killed them we considered them pigs." Women's bodies are one of the rewards of victory, and rape is an instrument to instill terror in the hearts of the conquered, to subjugate, intimidate, and demoralize them.

Susan Brownmiller in *Against Our Will*, and Peggy Reeves Sanday in *Female Power and Male Dominance* have demonstrated that rape has nothing to do with sexual urge and everything to do with power politics. In rape-prone societies, the act is a learned response rooted in social structures which encourage violent, aggressive and competi-tive behavior in boys and men.

Church and society give unwitting support to rape when they continue to delineate male and female, public and private spheres, as clearly distinct. Where the sexes are polarized and defined as opposite, where men are depicted as strong and powerful and women as weak and powerless, where rape and physical abuse are considered private, domestic affairs, sexual assault will continue unabated. It will become rare as power is better-distributed, sex roles are abolished, and the relations between the sexes are governed by real equality.

Economic exploitation is another, perhaps less dramatic, form of violence. The "feminization of poverty" has become a catchall phrase for a complex phenomenon which results in women's impoverishment. A growing proportion of the poor worldwide is composed of women, despite their high productivity in a wide range of human labor. Young women of color constitute 85% of the workforce in Third World countries in industries such as electronics, textiles and food processing. They are described as cheap, docile, nimble-fingered and well-suited to monotonous, repetitive work. Their availability attracts transnational companies, which benefit small segments of the population at the expense of the working poor. Women do this disgracefully underpaid work with no job security and no benefits, because they are socially, politically and economically vulnerable. Existing economic systems allow, and even encourage, this kind of exploitation.

On August 3, 1995, a stark example of the violent economic exploitation of women was uncovered in El Monte, California. Seventy Thai workers, almost all of them women, were being held behind bars and razor wire fences, forced to work long hours in the garment industry. They worked seven days a week, slept 16 to a room, and were paid $1.60 an hour to produce clothing bearing leading fashion labels, such as Macy's, Hecht's, and Filene's. Some had been beaten for attempting escape. This is but one example of the degradation of Asian women who are migrating to work in factories around the world. Their employment as domestics is equally rife with problems: exhausting hours, sexual harassment and abuse, poor living conditions, low wages. Their occupation as dancers and actors is scarcely better, and is often a disguise for sex trafficking.

Conditions in Central America are equally appalling. In El Salvador, women work 18 hours a day for $43.00 a week, making shirts under contract to GAP. American capitalists continue the oppression of the poor, carried out formerly by U.S.-backed Salvadoran death squads.[22]

In the United States, working conditions for women have steadily improved in this century; nevertheless, two-thirds of poor adults in our country are women; one-fifth of all elderly women are poor; and a persistent gap exists between wages for men and women for work of equal worth. These inequities affect not only women, but society at large. The cycle of poverty that affects entire families would be significantly interrupted if women were paid what similarly qualified men earn. Welfare reform might well begin with authentic equal employment opportunities and equal pay for work of equal value.

American women of every race and class face common problems, but there is a growing awareness of the variance in women's poverty. Middle-class women who have newly entered the ranks of the poor, women from a working-class background, African-American, Latina, Asian and Native American women, lesbians, older women and rural women – all experience poverty differently.[23] Virtually all women, however, suffer from society's failure to value women's and men's lives and work equally.

The lives of working women in the First and Third Worlds are related through their common exploitation. As industries that traditionally employ women move to the Third World in search of a cheap labor force, unemployment and poverty increase in the First World. But women worldwide are beginning to realize that they must not be pitted against one another; rather, they must focus their anger on the real culprit: multicorporations and colluding governments. And they must focus their minds and wills on breaking through the stereotypes in the division of labor which keep women concentrated in low-status, dead-end jobs.

It would be comforting to think that the church was leading the way, creating new models in the area of women's employment. And in fact, since Vatican II, discrimination against women has decreased and compensation has improved. Many more opportunities for ministry have opened up for women. They serve now in greater numbers in parish and diocesan ministries, often in positions that used to be reserved to the male clergy. Unfortunately, however, patterns of unjust compensation and discrimination persist. Many women church employees work without contracts, are arbitrarily fired, and are excluded from decision-making that affects their ministry. It would be a welcome relief if church authorities were to give more attention to this kind of injustice and to the sin that condemns women to poverty, malnutrition and illiteracy, and less to issues concerned with women's decisions concerning reproduction. Women will be freer to make well-informed and humane decisions about child-bearing when they enjoy economic independence and security. Which leads us to the thorny question of reproductive rights.

The Ethics of Reproductive Rights

The question of the control of women's reproductive capacity has been a hot and troubled one since the rebirth of the women's movement in the late 60s. The "Pill" afforded women more control than they previously had ever enjoyed, and the morality of its use is scarcely questioned now. The Catholic Church continues to condemn artificial contraception, and to teach that those who practice it are guilty of serious sin, but Catholics now generally avail themselves of this method of family planning with little sense of culpability or remorse.

The issue of abortion is more complex, despite extreme and insistent voices in both the pro-life and pro-choice camps, which attempt to reduce it to a simple matter of murder or to a simple question of a woman's individual right. Less extreme elements on either side of the issue share common ground in their respect for human life, but pro-lifers focus on the absolute right-to-life of the fetus, while pro-choice advocates insist on the need to weigh pre-natal life against the fully existent life of the woman who bears it.

The moral absolutism of the Vatican stance and of the pro-life forces of various denominations seems blind or unfeeling in light of the actual facts of real women's lives. Women still live in a context of male dominance, in which their social and political power is limited; in some parts of the world, this limitation is severe. Women constitute the bulk of those suffering poverty, but it is they who are expected to care for and rear children. They are more likely than men to be illiterate, and they are less likely than men to have access to adequate health care. These and other factors, such as sexual violence, forced marital coitus, lack of sex education and contraceptive failure help account for unwanted pregnancy.[24] In countries such as Brazil, where abortion is illegal, poor women resort to unsafe abortion methods, ranging from the use of hangers or poisonous herbs to operations in second-rate clinics, from which they often emerge mortally infected. Clandestine clinics, whether for working-class or upper-class women, provide an underworld economy which benefits few, other than those who control that economy.

For reasons such as these, more and more Catholics who accept the Church's teaching on the morality of abortion, nevertheless favor its legalization. Sr. Ivone Gebara, a gifted Brazilian theologian who was recently silenced by Vatican authorities, declared in an October 1993 interview for *Veja* that abortion should be a mother's choice and should be legalized. Acknowledging the violence of abortion, she believes that women make that traumatic choice only when obliged by circumstances. State-enforced anti-abortion policy does not deter them, and there is little evidence that the criminalization of abortion has had pro-life consequences anywhere. A report issued in Brazil, where abortion is illegal, estimates that for every 100 births, there are 44 abortions.

If anti-abortion laws don't work, what will? The alleviation of women's poverty and illiteracy, the encouragement of men to accept responsibility in the care and nurturance of their children, and effective sex education – everything, in fact, designed to enhance women's well-being, as Harrison points out, will minimize the necessity of abortion.[25] Meanwhile, perhaps the acrimonious and fruitless attempts of pro-lifers and advocates of pro-choice to persuade one another to change their basic positions can be transformed into mutual respect, based on the recognition of some common ground. Perhaps some agreement can be reached on the need to find a compromise between abortion on demand at any point in a pregnancy, on the one hand, and a rigid moral absolutism that masks the complex realities of real women's lives on the other.

The service rendered by feminists in various religious traditions in this disputed area of reproductive rights is their insistence on the right of women to bodily integrity. The fact that their voices are beginning to be heard was demonstrated at the Fourth U.N. Conference on Women, held in Beijing in September 1995. A section of the *Platform for Action* that issued from the Conference reads:

> Sexual rights include the individual's right to have control over and decide freely on matters related to her or his sexuality, free of coercion, discrimination and violence. Equal relationships between women and men in matters of sexual relations and reproduc-

tion, including full respect for the physical integrity of the human body, require mutual consent and willingness to accept responsibility for the consequences of sexual behavior.[26]

Freedom from coercion, discrimination and violence applies to forced pregnancy, forced abortion, forced sterilization and rape. The statement adopted at Beijing solidified and extended the sexual rights affirmed at Cairo in 1994. The document will not assure these rights, but it gives women a base from which to apply pressure on governments around the world. The Vatican itself seemed to recognize the grassroots support that the proposal enjoyed among the majority of the U.N. delegates and the NGO representatives, and to realize that an effort to roll back gains made in Cairo or to continue to oppose further progress at Beijing were doomed to failure.

The full recognition of women's sexual rights, which does not preclude a profound respect for motherhood, will cease to be an issue as women's real equality is progressively translated into economic, political and social terms everywhere: in America's ghettos, Africa's villages, Europe's parliaments, Latin America's barrios and China's countryside.

Ecology and Women

Ecology is another concern that has attracted the attention of women, and it is one of several areas where women's spirituality and ethics intersect. We have seen that reverence for the earth and a sense of the interconnectedness of all life permeate women's approach to God and to things of the spirit. This attentiveness to the beauty and sacredness of each interdependent part of creation renders women especially sensitive to what Elizabeth A. Johnson refers to as the sins of biocide, ecocide and geocide.[27]

The terrifying litany of the effects of ecological devastation are by now familiar to us: soil erosion and salination, the poisoning of the food chain, the depletion of marine life and the diminishment of plant and animal species through radiation and chemical pollution, the shrinking of forests, the expanding ozone hole, which has grown to twice the size of the continental United States, the greenhouse effect, drought and the sinking of water tables.

The insight that feminists have brought to the struggle for ecological sanity is this: the domination and liberation of women and nature are intimately linked. The abusive exploitation of nature will not stop until the destructive marginalization of women stops. Elizabeth A. Johnson writes:

> Within a sexist system the true identity of both women and the earth are skewed. Both are commonly excluded from the sphere of the sacred; both are routinely taken for granted and ignored, used and discarded, even battered and "raped," while nevertheless they do not cease to give birth and sustain life.[28]

The same patriarchal dualism that arranges supposed polar opposites in hierarchical pairs is at work here, distorting the relationship between God and creatures, men and women, human beings and the earth, nature and culture. Long accustomed to thinking that a Supremely Other Ruler stood at the apex of a pyramid that descended through angels, man, woman, animals, plants and non-sentient things, and assuming that those on the bottom rungs existed to serve and glorify those further up, we are now awakening to the dangers inherent in this imaginary arrangement. We sense the urgent need to recast this scenario and to rearrange its elements in a kind of circle dance. In the new arrangement, God joins us instead of looking down from a faraway throne; men and women, rich and poor, and people of every color, race and ethnic group form the circle and enjoy equal respect; their creative steps add to the energy of the dance. White men step out of the center, where their task was assumed to be to direct and control the dancers. All of the dancers, aware of their collusion in the earth's destruction, seek now to tread lightly and respectfully upon it and to be in right relationship with all that the earth sustains.

This right relationship includes a recognition of the profound communion that joins us to earth, sun, sea, sky, mountains, deserts, plants, animals and each other. We must imagine ourselves not at the helm of the universe, but as an integral part of it; not as the primary movers assigned to subdue the earth, but as derivative of the earth, in large measure dependent on its smooth functioning, and at the same time bearing a responsibility to care for it. Mystics have always experienced this oneness, this kinship with all that is. Cosmology, biology, physics and chemistry now bring scientific affirmation to their religious sensitivity. All creation is organically, chemically linked, and if we are to survive, we can no longer favor human life in a way that compromises or destroys other modes of existence.

Feminist ethics resonates well with both the spiritual sensibility of the mystics and the insights of contemporary science. What feminists have added to the dialogue is an emphasis on the centrality of relationships which are non-dualistic and non-patriarchal, and an insistence on the links that join the oppression of nature with other forms of oppression. Their reimaging of God as being as close to us as friend or lover has upset the chain of control and command which began with God and moved on down the pyramid, justifying man's domination of woman, and human domination of the earth. Lois K. Daly, in an exploration of the connections that link ecology, reverence for life and feminine ethics, points out that theologians like Carter Heyward and Sallie McFague, by articulating an ethics of justice, healing and companionship have enriched the discussion and the agenda for action surrounding the ecological crisis.[29]

Transforming Values: Love and Friendship

To speak of non-dualistic and non-patriarchal relation-ships, to seek relationships at all levels that are based on equality, mutual respect and nurturance, is to place love and friendship at the center of feminist ethics. Eleanor Humes Haney writes:

> To make friendship central is both to transform power relations that most often hold between individuals, groups, and people and the earth, and to be a par-ticipant in that transformation.[30]

The power dynamics that too often obtain in both personal and political relationships are those of control on the one hand, and fear and dependence on the other. And victims, whether battered wives or individuals or nations that are economically exploited, are often blamed for their own condition, while the powerful cloak their activity under the wraps of high moral purpose. The transformation Haney and other feminist ethicists have in mind entails a rejection of relationships based on coercive power, exploitation, authoritarian command and paternalistic condescension.

Female friendship ordinarily avoids these destructive forms of relationship. A constant and comforting phenomenon throughout history, friendship among women has become more open and more profound as women have found less need to compete for men once thought of as superior and once necessary as a means of support. Mary Hunt, in her book *Fierce Tenderness*, explores female friendship for its potential as a model for relationship among all of the elements of God's creation.[31] Based on mutual empowerment, friendship among women, in Hunt's view, encompasses love, embodiment and spirituality; generativity is its hallmark.

Female friendship can, furthermore, serve as a model for male-female friendship, and for male-male friendship, if it demonstrates an ability on each woman's part to listen, speak, be heard and respond, if it balances independence and responsibility, if it leads to solidarity with the entire human community, and strengthens each in her work for justice.

But can the kind of love, nurturance and care that is sought and accepted in personal relations and the private domain really be translated into the public, political realm? Are they valid, human activities, or are they somehow unrealistic and unmanly? Are competition, war and callous self-interest the lamentable but necessary ingredients of the "real world?" Feminists like Christine Gudorf don't think so. She analyzes the notion that ". . . impulses of the heart that govern our private lives are not . . . adequate for political decisions," and finds it wanting.[32] She points out that giving priority to the neediest child, friend or neighbor is taken for granted in the private sphere. Private morality supports, for instance, allotting a disproportionate share of a family's health budget for a child needing surgical correction of a birth defect or cure of a debilitating disease. It does not entail the kind of misplaced pity, she points out, that exempts a child from normal family rules in a way that would suggest that what is special about the child is her lameness. Gudorf believes that this kind of preferential treatment in the private domain can be applied to the political arena, and can justify a preferential option for the poor. This option is realistic and healthy, she argues, when it is about ". . . removing the poverty of the affected individuals with the goal of making them whole and restoring them to equality and participation in the human community."[33] Here, once again, feminist theory cuts through divisions that keep private and public moralities in separate categories, and by so doing makes it possible to envision more benevolent political and economic systems.

An ethic of love and friendship is obviously not a new one. It is deeply embedded in the gospel, and was lived out by Jesus and his followers, men and women alike. Seen today through women's eyes, however, love and friendship take on new dimensions. They serve as foundation of the hope that love for our authentic selves, loving respect for every creature, loving wonder in the face of earth's beauty, and joy in the knowledge that a complex and mysterious web joins all of this, may yet save us and the planet from further destruction.

Endnotes

1. Margaret Farley, "New Patterns of Relationship: Beginnings of a Moral Revolution," *Theological Studies* 36/4 (1975): 627-46.
2. See Carole Pateman, "'The Disorder of Women': Women, Love, and the Sense of Justice," *Ethics* 91 (October 1980): 20-34.
3. "The Human Situation: a Feminine Viewpoint," *Journal of Religion* 40 (April 1990): 100-112.
4. See Rosemarie Tong, *Feminine and Feminist Ethics* (Belmont, CA: Wadsworth Pub. Co., 1993), ch. 1.
5. Margaret A. Farley, "Feminist Ethics," in *The Westminster Dictionary of Christian Ethics*, 1986.
6. *Ibid.*, 231.
7. Seyla Benhabib, "The Generalized and the Concrete Other: The Kohlberg-Gilligan Controversy and Feminist Theory," in *Feminism as Critique,* eds. Seyla Benhabib and Drucilla Cornell (Minneapolis: University of Minnesota Press, 1987), 83.
8. *Ibid.*
9. Quoted in Daphne Hampson, *Theology and Feminism* (Cambridge, Mass.: Basil Blackwell, Ltd., 1990), 126.
10. See Barbara Hilkert Andolsen's article "Agape in Feminist Ethics," *Journal of Religious Ethics* 9 (1981): 69-83.
11. *Ibid.*, 70.
12. *A Feminist Ethics of Risk,* (Minneapolis: Fortress Press, 1990), 111.
13. "The Politics of Paradise: Augustine's Exegesis of Genesis 1-3 versus that of John Chrysostom," *Harvard Theological Review* 78:1-2 (1985): 89.
14. Theology for Skeptics (Minneapolis: Fortress Press, 1995), 25.
15. Creative Disobedience (Cleveland: The Pilgrim Press, 1995), 52.
16. *Making the Connections* (Boston: Beacon Press, 1985), 3-21.
17. "Letter to Women," *Origins* 25 (27 July 1995): 137, 139-143.
18. Tong, 100.

19. *Pure Lust,* (Boston: Beacon Press, 1984), 274-280.

20. The "Foreword" in Linda Bell's *Rethinking Ethics in the Midst of Violence* (Boston: Rowman & Littlefield, 1993), xi-xii.

21. Gyn/Ecology: The Metaethics of Radical Feminism (Boston: Beacon Press, 1978).

22. See Frances Wright, "Union fights 'peonage' in U.S., El Salvador," *World,* 12 August 1995.

23. The book *For Crying Out Loud* takes into account these differences and offers some explanations – economic, cultural and sociological – for the fact of women's poverty in the United States.

24. See Beverly Wildung Harrison, "Theology and Morality of Procreative Choice," in *On Moral Medicine, Theological Perspectives in Medical Ethics,* ed. Stephen E. Lammers (Grand Rapids: William B. Eerdmans, 1987), 426-427.

25. *Ibid.,* 431.

26. Chapter IV, article 97.

27. Women, Earth, and Creator Spirit (New York: Paulist Press,1993), 65.

28. *Ibid.* 2.

29. See "Ecofeminism, Reverence for Life, and Feminine Theological Ethics," in *Feminist Theological Ethics,* ed. Lois K. Daly (Louisville: Westminster John Knox Press, 1994), 295-313.

30. "What is Feminist Ethics? A Proposal for Continuing Discussion," *The Journal of Religious Ethics* 8/1 (Spring 1980): 118.

31. *Fierce Tenderness,* A Feminist Theology of Friendship, (New York: Crossroad, 1991), ch. 4.

32. *Victimization, Examining Christian Complicity* (Philadelphia: Trinity Press International, 1992), 35.

33. *Ibid.,* 37.

Chapter 3

Women and Language

Our age is clearly fascinated with language. Some hold that language and reality are synonymous; language actually *constitutes* reality. For others, language is merely a set of sounds or symbols; true reality lies beyond language. Aristotle found in language the key to what makes us human. William Burroughs muses that "Language is a virus from outer space," suggesting that it is something mysterious that invades and infects us. Some tell us that language not only expresses our experience, it is virtually indistinguishable from that experience. Others demonstrate how language is a tool of social and psychological exclusion. And many see language, images and symbols as instruments, not only of power, but of transformation.

Reflection and debate about language has spilled over from the academy into the media, the workplace, the courtrooms, and the pews and pulpits of our churches. What might once have been dismissed as mere semantics or "pronoun envy" (in relation to the pseudo-generic "he") or harmless racial epithets or playful flirting is now subject to subtle and serious analysis. Politically correct language may still be the butt of jokes that ridicule and trivialize the painfully real issues underlying it, but the fact is our language is changing because our consciousness of identity and of social reality is changing. Our relationships – among classes, different races and ethnic groups, between women and men, between us and God – are changing. These shifts inevitably affect the way we talk.

Sociolinguists are fond of pointing out that while our experience, attitudes, and behavior influence our language, language itself is a powerful force in shaping our self-concept and the way we view the world. In a very real sense, the limits of our language define the limits of our thought and the horizons of our world. There is, then, a kind of circular movement by which one's personal language, thought and experience constantly interact. On a larger screen, there is a connection as well between language and social change, and it, too, is circular. In this sense it is not particularly profitable to argue about whether changes in language actually bring about change in social practices and institutions or whether linguistic changes are a symptom of these institutional changes. Just as, in another sphere, it is futile to spend time asking, "Does the way we speak to and of God change our concept of God, or do altered ways of thinking about God require changes in the language?" Social institutions, interpersonal relations, language and God-talk all change together. The way we talk, our efforts to communicate, are part of a complex set of social processes that affect every sector of our lives. Our speech and our silences, the way we speak and the way we're spoken to, the words used to describe us, the words we use to describe others, the words we use to describe ourselves: all of this shapes our experience, and all of it shifts as we reevaluate and reassess our experience.

Language and Gender

The women's movement has ignited a revolution in the way women think of themselves and of their experience and in the speech they use to describe their awakening. The movement, and the feminist critique that accompanies it, has affected the field of linguistics as it has affected every discipline, prodding researchers to pose questions never raised before.

To the extent that male scholars from an earlier period considered the question of gender and language, they based their conclusions less on empirical research than on stereotypical notions of what constitutes male and female speech. Otto Jespersen in an influential study entitled *Language: Its Nature, Development and Origin* (1922) referred to English as the "language of grown up men," and felt that women's languid, insipid, indirect and ineffective speech constituted a threat to the "vigour and vividness" (provided by males) of the mother tongue.[1] He credited men with language innovation, and characterized women's expression as refined, euphemistic and hyperbolic. Other linguists reinforced the idea that language is a male preserve and that women's speech is deficient. Early feminist reflections on language tended to be ignored. Thorne, Kramarae and Henley point out that in the first half of the century, women like Charlotte Carmichael Stopes, Elsie Clews Parsons and Mary Beard were already questioning the effect of the generic masculine on women's freedom, the linguistic double-standard that implied the superiority of men, and the effect of sex-linked taboos on language use.[2]

Their questions would be taken up again in the 70s. The prolonged battle over the use of "he" and "man" as generic terms meant to include girls and women is now virtually won. It is widely recognized that this usage and other rules laid down by grammarians centuries ago functioned to maintain women in a secondary position, if not to render them invisible. There was the rule of male precedence, for instance, set down in 1560 by one Mr. Wilson. He raised to the level of prescriptive grammar the usage of naming males first, because he said, ". . . the worthier is preferred and set before. As a man is sette before a woman."[3] And so we have *Mr. and Mrs., he and she, his and hers, men and women, Adam and Eve, Abraham and Sarah, Dick and Jane, Bill and Hillary,* and the other endless combinations that teach women their place.

Eighteenth-century grammarians decided that number should take precedence over gender, and their rule was strengthened by an Act of Parliament in 1850, which outlawed the use of "they" or "their" for sex-indeterminable references. "Everybody" and "somebody" became unambiguously male: everybody should say his prayers; somebody should speak his mind; a voter must follow his conscience. In coed schools each student was to raise his hand, do his homework, and be loyal to his school. And there was "the doctor, he . . .," "the Christian, he . . .," "the Congressman, he . . . ." Male grammarians and Members of Parliament had dictated that "he" stood for "she" when necessary in these and countless other instances. Women were left to wonder when "he" and "man" meant specific male beings, and when these terms were meant to embrace both sexes. A woman reading Oliver Wendell Holmes' statement, "A man's mind, stretched by a new idea, can never go back to its original dimensions," *could* read herself into the sentence, but she might wonder if Holmes really intended for her to be there. It isn't clear. What became clear to many, however, is that the generic masculine was ambiguous and discriminatory, and that the English language had an androcentric bias that reinforced male domination.

Efforts to correct the bias, although still occasionally the subject of derisive humor, have paid off. The singular "they" and "their," which never really passed out of the vernacular, have been granted grammatical acceptability. Gender considerations have finally taken precedence over agreement in number. Publishers of children's books instruct their authors to "degender" titles, occupations and personality traits.[4] Non-sexist language guidelines are a staple of publishing houses, and contemporary authors have, by and large, found graceful ways around what only a few years ago were considered impossible barriers. Of course, those who "get it," those whose consciousness has changed in regard to women's presence in the world and to male-female relationships, don't need guidelines. Inclusive language flows easily from an inclusive mentality.

Analysis of the relationship between language and gender has gone well beyond the notion of non-sexist or inclusive language and the discriminatory effects of pseudo-generic nouns and pronouns. It touches on the sensitive areas of politics and power, on the construction of language and the use of language as power tools.

Language and Power

Definitions of power usually include the notion of a capacity to influence others, to produce effects on them not always of their own choosing. Authoritative, persuasive, even manipulative speech is one obvious means of doing this. And although research on the relationship of language and power is at an early stage, some linguists are convinced that ". . . consideration of either ultimately entails the other."[5]

Although power is often represented as negative and repressive (perhaps because, in the wrong hands, it often is), those who study its workings point out that it can be used to good purpose, that it can be nurturing and beneficent. To understand power at all, we must study it as part of the social context within which it operates. Power is essentially relational. Elizabeth Janeway has written of the *Powers of the Weak*, the power of those on the margins, and reminds us that these are the groups that have historically brought about revolutionary social change. The unequal distribution of power and influence can be affected by the bargaining power of "the weak" or by their refusal to submit, and this, indeed, is the classic way that power relations are changed. African-Americans won civil liberties and women got the vote, not through the gracious and gentlemanly bestowal of these basic rights by lawmakers, but because the marginalized raised their voices, struggled and suffered for them.

Language as an instrument of power is at the disposal of all. But at that point where language, gender and power intersect, feminists have convincingly demonstrated that men's advantage has been overwhelming. Research in the areas of vocabulary and interactive speech among women and men, for instance, has unearthed some revealing patterns. Dale Spender refers to studies done in the mid-70s that suggest a ". . . systematic, semantic derogation of women."[6] A few indicators:

- Words for males are more numerous and more positive than words for females.

- Of the smaller stock of words assigned to women, 220 describe a sexually promiscuous woman (as compared to 20, mainly laudatory, for sexually promiscuous males).

- Words associated with females, originally neutral or honorable, tend to become "pejorated." (e.g., bitch, dame, mistress, courtesan, madame).

- Boys' names that become popular as girls' names (e.g., Leslie, Beverley, Evelyn), lose their appeal and are no longer considered suitable for males. The process does not operate in reverse.

- Th ere is no female equivalent for the words "virility" or "potency" – words that would describe women as strong and sexually healthy beings. Women, as described in the male lexicon, are either "frigid" or "nymphomaniacs."

In a patriarchal system, furthermore, women's speech has been devalued, trivialized as gossip, small talk, silly chatter. Like children's talk, it can be easily interrupted. In mixed-gender groups, men typically initiate topics of conversation, and despite prevailing opinion and numerous jokes to the contrary, they apparently talk more than women. While women pick up male-initiated topics, men tend to let women's topics die. In classrooms, boys or men are called on more; their questions and comments get more time and consideration. These commonly observed phenomena point to unequal access to speech, and hint at a kind of verbal exclusion that translates into social and psychological exclusion.

But the male-dominant idiom has consequences that go beyond questions of vocabulary and interactive speech patterns. The latter are not insignificant; they contribute to one's sense of identity, one's place in the social hierarchy. But at a deeper level, the question of language, gender and power revolves around the fact that men have named and defined *their* experience and presented it as *human* experience. It is men's life, culture and speech that have been central to public arenas. Their questions have shaped research in every field; their answers based on their world view – the view principally of white, wealthy, heterosexual men – have set the parameters of knowledge. Men's virtual monopoly on naming, defining and interpreting – the most powerful of speech acts – has been a means of creating a world whose center they occupy. From that center they speak a language that enhances and justifies their power. Their speech keeps prevailing power dynamics in place; it functions to reinforce their control of church, educational and legal systems, government and industry. Clearly, the English language, its images and metaphors, are closely tied to a patriarchal social structure; they reflect its social values and relationships. But all of this is changing.

Women's Silence/Women's Speech

If women's speech has been devalued, her silence has been considered golden. In Fennimore, Wisconsin, there is a restaurant named "The Silent Woman." The prominent sign outside features a headless woman, garbed in 19th-century dress and holding a tray. Here is the perfect servant: female, headless, mute. Less-graphic examples could be endlessly multiplied. There is the pastor who told the Sister on his pastoral team not to speak during a parish meeting because it was important that they present a "united front." There are the scriptural injunctions, such as:

> Let a woman learn in silence with full submissiveness.
> I do not allow any woman to teach or to exercise authority over a man; she is to remain silent, for Adam was formed first, then Eve. . . . (2 Timothy, 2:11-14)

The authors of *After Eden* tell us that Ambrose Bierce's *The Devil's Dictionary* defines woman as "the animal which can be taught not to talk."[7] They outline the devices used to punish women in colonial America who dared speak out or speak too much: they were held under water, publicly gagged, or fitted into iron frames furnished with metal bits for their mouths. Dale Spender speculates that a "talkative" woman may be one who talks as much as a man; she may even be one who dares to talk at all![8]

Adrienne Rich reminds us, though, that "In a world where language and naming are power, silence is oppression, is violence."[9] And Audre Lorde says starkly:

> I was going to die, if not sooner then later, whether or not I had ever spoken myself. My silences had not protected me. Your silence will not protect you.[10]

Messages like these emboldened women, who began with increasing courage to define themselves, to speak themselves, to forge a new language that voiced their experience. Early in the game Nelle Morton described the slow but inevitable explosion that occurred as women touched into their own pain and anger, and as they heard one another with new ears into a new speech.[11] In consciousness-raising groups all over the country, women strained against the limits of a pervasively male language system that hid or blunted the reality of their own experience. Morton in 1972 wrote:

> One may safely predict the consciousness to acceler-
> ate, increase in power, until a new language of the
> *full human* experience begins to express itself all
> over.[12]

The last quarter of a century bears abundant, amazing and eloquent witness to this prediction.

One manifestation of new naming is the addition of words like "sexism" and "sexual harassment" to our vocabulary. The arrangements and behavior described by these terms are not new, but giving them a name that emerges from women's feelings and from their stronger stance *is* new; it throws the behavior into an entirely new light. A Russian (male) television commentator could still dismiss Yeltsin's much-publicized pinching of a secretary at a 1995 U.N. meeting as good-natured horseplay ("He must have been in a good mood.") American audiences, especially after the Clarence Thomas/Anita Hill hearings, the jail sentence served by Mike Tyson, and the resignation of former Senator Packwood because of charges of sexual harassment, looked at it differently. Women's daring to speak out, their refusal to accept the blame and the guilt for being prey to male aggression, has turned the tables.

The revolution in language encompasses more than the naming of what women have experienced as negative. Women are constructing a positive, powerful language as well. Its sources, once more, are in the authentic naming of their own experience, in the validation of one another's speech and experience, and in using the tools of scholarship from their stance at the margin. Mary Daly has done this, at one and the same time with deadly seriousness and playful inventiveness. Her work of liberating the construction of knowledge from its male subjectivity has been done, in part, through a recasting of language. She has reclaimed words (like hag, crone and spinster), redefined words (like glamour, fashion, penis envy), discovered words, made words up, exposed word reversals, created word reversals, coined new expressions, and lured her readers into "word-webs" where they find themselves gazing into wild, unexpected possibilities.[13] This word play grows out of a changed consciousness, and it leads to further and deeper transformations in the ways that women perceive reality.

Another aspect of women's liberation of speech has been their talk of formerly taboo topics. Menstruation, pregnancy, nursing, menopause, when named at all were, in the past, named by men. Looked upon by them as strange, mysterious, debilitating, even disgusting functions of the female body, women themselves were ambiguous about the functions that marked the cycles of their lives. Were these functions, indeed, unclean and unmentionable? Or were they named so because they differed from the presumably standard norm of men's physiology? Accepting, loving, honoring their own female bodies, women have found ways of speaking of them as sources of power and creative energy. New rituals of initiation into menstruation enable girls on the threshold of womanhood to see it as gift. Naming their own experience of abortion, birth, pregnancy and nursing among women who have shared these experiences allows women to explore freely and authentically the range of emotions that accompany these events. And women have discovered in menopause much more than an entrance into dull, sexless old age. Whatever loss may be associated with this period in their lives, women have also found in post-menopausal life a period of new activity, freedom, wisdom and joy.

The notion of women as men's sexual toy is still around, but women are more and more strenuously rejecting it. Ads depicting women as dangerous seductresses associated with everything from Taco Bell products to America OnLine services strike most women, and one hopes most men, as foolishly outdated, although still enraging. Women are not rejecting their sexuality, but in defining it themselves they are moving beyond the limits of the traditional roles of virgin, whore, or (tamed) wife and mother, and finding in the erotic a resource that strengthens and replenishes them. Audre Lorde writes:

> We have been taught to suspect this resource, vilified, abused, and devalued within western society. On the one hand, the superficially erotic has been encouraged as a sign of female inferiority; on the other hand, women have been made to suffer and to feel both contemptible and suspect by virtue of its existence.[14]

In renaming the erotic, women find in it a depth of feeling, satisfaction, and wholeness related to all of the vital aspects of their lives: their sexuality, work, spirituality and search for knowledge. Lorde asserts that this understanding bears no resemblance to the "plasticized sensation" or the pornographic representations which men have peddled as eroticism and which have tempted women to suppress their erotic demands. But in yielding to this temptation, women reduce their capacity for deep feeling, deep satisfaction and deep joy. In the healing power of speech and of self-definition, women are reclaiming all of this.

As we saw in the context of feminist ethics, women are also using their voices to bring to public notice an analysis of the dynamics of personal relationships between women, between men, and between women and men. At first focusing on the gender hierarchy that exists in male-female relations, feminist thinkers have since broadened the scope of their analysis and brought new moral dimensions to the understanding of love, care and friendship. They have enriched classical thought on friendship with reflection from women's perspective, and have insisted on the need to transform human relations not just for women's benefit, but for the full flourishing of the human race. In the process, women are speaking of their love and friendship for one another. This frank relishing of women's company required a refusal of women to look upon themselves any longer as competitors for the favor of men, or as beings whose very identity derived from their relations with men. In overcoming the physical and psychological barriers that kept them isolated and separated from one another, women are finding in each other sources of affirmation and delight. "Gyn/affection" is the word created by Janice Raymond to describe loving relations between women, whether sexual or non-sexual. She defines it as ". . . the state of influencing, acting upon, moving, and impressing, and of being influenced, acted upon, moved and experienced by other women."[15] This mutual influencing, this mutual self-revelation encourages women to plumb the full extent of their pain and of their power. In the process, the one is transformed into the other, and women begin to experience and enjoy a new-found strength.

The unfolding of a new consciousness in women, and the expression of their newly-found identity in new speech, has affected every sphere of life: domestic arrangements, education, literature, law, media, medicine, and of course, religion and worship.

Women and Religious Language

Numerous committees and commissions are hard at work all over the English-speaking world, producing inclusive-language translations of the Bible, lectionaries, hymns and prayer books. The challenge facing them is formidable. They must try at one and the same time to remain faithful to the Christian tradition, respect contemporary sensibilities, and produce texts in language that has some rhythm and grace. Their brave efforts have not been spared caustic criticism. In regard to the *Inclusive Language Lectionary: Readings for Year A*, James J. Kilpatrick wrote in the *Washington Post* of October 21, 1983:

> It is probably a waste of time, energy and indignation to denounce the latest efforts to castrate the Holy Bible, but vandalism of this magnitude ought not to go unremarked.

The choice of the verb "castrate" is telling. More recently, in the October 2, 1995 issue of *The New Yorker*, in an article entitled "Scripture Rescripted," Anthony Lane pans the Oxford inclusive version of the New Testament and Psalms.[16] His objections, and he makes them with acerbic wit, are largely based on the new version's lack of artistic merit; but he argues as well that the deep religious sense and the sheer force of faith that mark earlier versions, such as the King James' edition, collapse here under the weight of political correctness. Bishop Donald W. Trautman, until recently the head of the Catholic Bishops' Committee on the Liturgy, rejects the translation outright and does not approve its use. The editorial board of the new translation, it would seem, put its main emphasis on updating the language and removing the androcentric bias of biblical texts – a worthy and necessary task – but their efforts demonstrate once more the difficulties inherent in their self-imposed assignment.

The fact is, the scriptures were written by men in a male-dominant culture. In many instances, the word is addressed to men. Almost any page of the Bible serves to illustrate this fact. The Book of Proverbs, for instance, is addressed to the young and inexperienced man; in it a father gives instruction to his son, and we read of arrogant men, wise men, greedy men, old men, shrewd men, lowly men, just men. The few times that a woman or women appear (as mothers, wives, prostitutes, and adulteresses), they are seen through the eyes of men. God is spoken of throughout the Bible mainly in masculine images: Lord, Father, King, Judge, Warrior. The language of the Bible flows, after all, from a certain world view – one that assumes male privilege, dominant-subordinate social relations, and hierarchical power models. Can this really be turned around, or must we read these pages in their historical context as mirrors of a patriarchal culture that is slowly dying? Can we, at the same time, read around, under, over, and beyond patriarchal assumptions to find the words of justice and mercy and life that continue to nourish us? Is our nameless God, the Holy One, lurking there somewhere beneath the male garb?

Christian feminists, keenly sensitive to the androcentric bias of scripture and to the absence or distortion of women's experience in its pages, have nevertheless found in the Bible a liberating message that undercuts its patriarchal trappings. They are bringing out of the shadows and reinterpreting the women of the Bible. They are highlighting images of God that have been repressed or overlooked, and they are insisting that the proclamation of the Word be a word of salvation for *everyone.*

Elisabeth Schüssler Fiorenza, for example, in her book *In Memory of Her,* reads the story of Judith from a feminist perspective. She reminds us of Judith's determination not to become a victim, and her exhortation to her people to reject that role. She recalls the victory march in which Judith, crowned with garland leaves, leads the women of Israel in song and dance. In the same volume, Fiorenza points out how the earliest Jesus traditions perceive God as a God of gracious goodness, personified in female imagery as Sophia or Wisdom. This God is called sister, wife, mother, beloved and teacher. She offers life, rest, knowledge and salvation to those who accept her.

Fiorenza does not ignore or try to salvage misogynistic texts; she faces them squarely and recognizes their potential power as part of women's "subversive memory." On the other hand, she highlights the role of women in the early Christian missionary movement in a way that reveals them as initiators and leaders of the movement and not simply as the apostles' helpers. Women's history in the Bible emerges from Fiorenza's pen as the history of a discipleship of equals. Other scholars, too, have found in the pages of scripture an authoritative summons to women to assume their rightful place in the church. Working in accord with the most demanding standards of biblical study, Anne Carr, Sandra Schneiders, Phyllis Trible, Elizabeth Johnson and a host of others expose the futility of attempting to justify oppressive texts as representing the revelatory Word of God. They, at one and the same time, ". . . keep alive the memory of our foresisters' struggles and sufferings in patriarchal religion," and ". . . articulate the liberating experiences of women in biblical religion."[17] Through their reinterpretation and reconstruction, they open our eyes to a new reading of scripture and to fresh possibilities for the church of the future.

The Language of Worship

It is in the context of worship and public prayer that the ordinary Christian comes most often into contact with religious language and the language of scripture. The language in which we couch the prayer and worship of an assembled community not only expresses but helps to shape our concept of God, the relationship of God to church, and our relationships with one another. As these concepts changed in the wake of the Second Vatican Council, liturgical structure, practice, and language also changed. Women became more visible in liturgies as eucharistic ministers and readers, for instance; girls began to appear as altar servers in certain parishes; and language became more inclusive, acknowledging women's existence and experience.

Ruth Fox, a Benedictine religious, notes, however, that many women who figure prominently in scripture never made the cut when selections were made for readings at Mass.[18] For instance, mention of Phoebe, deacon of the church of Corinth, is eliminated from Paul's greetings. In the reading about the valiant woman in the Book of Proverbs, the faithful hear the verses that praise her as a worthy wife, but not those that laud her initiative, business acumen or wisdom. The prophet Miriam's sin and punishment is mentioned, but not the passage that names her as prophet. Deborah, prophet and judge, who accompanied her appointed general in victorious battle, is not mentioned at all.

Reference to Jesus' women disciples is often relegated to weekday readings, and the Easter Gospel stops just short of mentioning the tender encounter of Jesus and Mary Magdalen in the garden. Mary's exultant song, the Magnificat, is never read on a Sunday. We need not read these and other significant omissions as part of a dark plot to keep women invisible, but we must question the criteria of selection that deprive girls and women of acquaintance with their foremothers and the assembled Christian community of a vital part of their salvation history.

If revisions of liturgical rites failed to bring women's stories to the fore, they did, as acknowledged above, attempt to render liturgical language more inclusive. The ubiquitous "brothers," "sons," "forefathers" and "men" gave way in time to phrases in which women could find themselves. Women's alienation and anger, if not addressed in depth, was at least recognized, and the language of the liturgy began to be a little more faithful to the experience of the gathered community.

The difficulty and magnitude of the task of rendering liturgical language more inclusive and less discriminatory is outlined by J. Frank Henderson in his "ICEL and Inclusive Language."[19] The International Commission on English in the Liturgy recognized that the issue of inclusive and non-discriminatory language embraced racial and anti-semitic bias as well as gender bias, but language excluding women was their first priority and focus. It had to be addressed in a wide array of liturgical texts: various rites (e.g., anointing of the sick, funerals, commissioning of ministers), lection-aries, and the *Roman Missal*. The initial moves were minimal and cautious ones, and even these had to win the approval of the bishops' conferences, of which ICEL is an agency, and the approval of the Holy See. But in the course of a few years, it became evident that understanding of the issue deepened among the members and associate members of ICEL. They recognized that reform had to move beyond the simple elimination of pseudo-generics. Changes would have to take into account the connection between the language, symbols and images used in the liturgy, and the religious understanding and practice of the people of God. They acknowledged that women's absence in liturgical language effectively excluded them from full participation in the life of the Church, and that this exclusion impoverished the Christian community. And they noted that many women were experiencing a personal crisis in terms of Church life and worship, a crisis serious enough to prompt some to abandon corporate worship altogether.

ICEL has been maligned for its long-term commitment to liturgical language that is inclusive and that is free of texts that imply women's inferiority or subjection. But in spite of lack of support and strong opposition from some quarters, the Commission continues to provide leadership in this complex and crucially important area.[20]

The bishops' conferences of the United States and Canada immediately approved the eucharistic prayers changed according to the principles enunciated by ICEL. But Rome gave approval only to change "for all men" to "for all," postponing consideration of other inclusive language changes until the entire Missal was revised. It will come as no surprise that disaffected worshipping communities began to make their own textual changes, and that women continued to abandon corporate worship.

The God-Language Issue

> These are dark days if you happen to be God. Not only are the peoples of the earth writhing in sin, as per usual, and taking your name in vain, but some of them are wondering whether your name was the right one in the first place.[21]

This wry observation of Anthony Lane on the pages of The New Yorker reminds us that the question of naming God has moved out of the confines of bishops' conferences and academic circles and has caught the attention of the mass media. And no wonder. The question of inclusive language as it applies to the naming of Christian worshippers was difficult enough, but when the issue is extended to encompass the way we speak of God, the stakes are higher, the emotions more intensely engaged, and change proportionately more difficult to effect.

What is the problem? Mary Collins argues persuasively that the question of how we shall address God in public prayer is not a "woman's issue," the outgrowth of an amorphous, marginal social movement, but "a radical theological and ecclesial question."[22] She is right, of course. But, then, all of the questions raised by the women's movement ultimately touch broader issues. They touch the nerve centers of the human condition: power, ego, governance, social relations, right action, worship. The way we name and speak of God is, indeed, an ecclesial question and not simply a feminist agenda item, but the question was bound to evoke feminist exploration.

One of the earliest insights of the feminist movement was that the naming of God as male suggested that men somehow were made more in God's image than women. While men were associated with God, women were associated with sin and evil. This obviously had effects on how women and men perceived themselves and each other. It also affected the relative roles women and men would play in the church. ". . . men [are] granted power by the use of male referents to God, but women are denied legitimate power by the absence of female referents," notes Marjorie Procter-Smith.[23]

The exclusion of women from ordained ministry in the Catholic church effects a further distancing from power. The requirement that priests be male because they are "other Christs" puts a strange emphasis on Christ's maleness, and further distorts our understanding of God. The humanity shared equally by women and men, and assumed and redeemed by the second person of the Trinity, embraces both genders and renders both capable of sacramentally representing the Risen Christ – the true presider and ultimate intercessor at the eucharist.

Women theologians point out that clinging to God the Father as the one metaphor for God could suggest that the metaphor actually defines God's essence; it could suggest that God is literally a father. But this is idolatrous. In reminding us of this fact, contemporary women theologians are simply reiterating what theologians and mystics have said through the ages: God is not male, not female and not androgynous. *Every* name for God is simply a metaphor, an analogy, enabling us to speak of God and inviting us to reflect on some aspect of God's being. Reducing our images of God to exclusively male metaphors denies us access to the full beauty of God and to the full meaning of God's intervention in human affairs. When our language for God stresses sovereignty, absolute authority and rule over others, then God-language seems to support the raw drive for power and the master/servant relations that characterize patriarchal cultures. Women are not alone today in seeking a God who loves and liberates, who is exuberant and sublimely playful. Our age begs for a God who draws us into new understandings of power, mutuality, obedience, maturity, suffering, and our relations with one another and with the earth.

Representing this kind of God requires a broadening of our images of God. Although the preponderance of metaphors in scripture are masculine, feminine or female ones do find their place there: God as mother, midwife, homemaker, she-bear, mother eagle. If these female images have been buried in the theological, liturgical and homiletic tradition, Sandra Schneiders suggests that it is because men have told the story of God, and the story is ". . . the one which they wanted to hear as well as the one which kept them in power."[24]

ICEL wrestled with the matter of God-language, acknowledging that:

> . . . every effort should be made to use language that least distorts, narrows, or hampers our appreciation, understanding, experience, and relationship with God.[25]

A subcommittee, however, pointed out that ICEL's translation of the Latin missal had actually increased the use of the term Father. *Pater* had been used in only 21 out of 1400 collects in the Latin missal; ICEL's translations used it in 560 collects. While recommending that "Father" be retained in the Lord's prayer, Creed, baptismal formula, and doxologies, the subcommittee suggested that an explicit reason be given for use of the term "Father" if the term did not appear in the Latin translation. The subcommittee also recommended that a wider range of images and attributes be used for God in prayer texts, and that liturgical prayer make fuller use of the biblical tradition in its ways of addressing God. In 1987, the Advisory Committee of ICEL actually seemed to agree that, as a general rule, masculine pronouns should not be used for God, but this was not submitted to a general vote.[27] The issue was reopened more recently, indicating that the question of God-language will be a live and controversial one for the foreseeable future.

In the fall of 1994, the Vatican dealt a blow to efforts by the U.S. bishops to furnish an inclusive-language translation of the Bible. Although Rome's Worship Congregation had given approval in 1992, the doctrinal congregation, two years later, rescinded permission for the use of translations from the New Revised Standard Version of the Bible for public worship, giving no specific reasons for doing so. This decision calls into question the guidelines that the U.S. bishops adopted in 1990 for the use of inclusive language in scriptural texts intended for liturgical use. Bishop Trautman's plea that inclusive language was a necessity in American idiom and culture fell on deaf ears. For the moment, the United States bishops have agreed to temporarily accept Vatican recommendations for very limited changes. They will revisit the issue in five years.

These delays and setbacks are disillusioning. For increasing numbers of women the proposed changes, while welcome, are too timid, too long in coming, and too uneven in their application in various dioceses and parishes. They turn to feminist or women's liturgies either to supplement official liturgies or to replace them.

Feminist Liturgies

During retreats given by and for women, and at regular gatherings during which women meet to share their faith and their lives, women are creating liturgies that better express their experience and their view of God and of all reality. Mary Collins identifies five principles that guide intentionally feminist liturgies: they ". . . ritualize relation-ships that emancipate and empower women"; they are designed by the worshipers themselves and not by liturgical experts; they critique patriarchal liturgies; they use distinctive ritual symbols and strategies; and they ". . . produce liturgical events, not liturgical texts." [28]

Women at feminist liturgies use scriptural and other readings of their own choosing. They often select stories from the Bible that focus on women, and reflect on these texts from their own perspective. If the scene is one that is hostile to women, it becomes part of their "subversive memory," and their ritual seeks to exorcise its harmful effects. More commonly the texts chosen depict women's compas-sion, prophetic power, wisdom, intimacy with God and with Jesus, and affirm those present in their effort to create a more humane world.

A feminist liturgy often incorporates periods of medi-tative silence, a time for centering. When it is time to speak, the women use language that is naturally inclusive. And they use means of communication other than words: images, symbols and myths that connect with women's lives, memory and history, and that reveal God in many guises. They alternate leadership roles, and call upon all to design and participate in ritual expressions of solidarity and of com-munion with God and of all creation. These rituals often involve body movement, simple gestures or dance that remind the participants of the divine dwelling within them and within all God has made.

At feminist liturgies, women can reflect on and ritualize experiences specific to them: menarche, pregnancy, giving birth, menopause. This sacralizing of women's embodied selves delivers them from both the romanticization of these functions and the fear and taboos surrounding them. Rosemary Radford Ruether points to the need to recognize in liturgical settings other realities of women's lives as well: miscarriage, abortion, divorce, rape, wife-battering. Women who have experienced these things often feel distanced from human communities and from God. They need a healing that has its source in a supportive community and in the assurance of God's faithful love.[29] Healing rites of this kind do not find a place in the church's traditional ceremonies.

Feminist liturgies normally take place in settings other than chapels and churches. The architecture of the latter, beautiful and inspiring as it often is, helps to maintain relations of domination: elevated space for the presider, for instance, toward whom all face while looking at the back of one another's heads; pews to facilitate worshippers' kneeling (as one kneels in the presence of lords and kings), while the presider stands. At feminist liturgies women typically sit informally in a circle. The seating stresses the equality of all present and permits participants to see one another's faces.

Other elements of feminist liturgies contribute to the atmosphere of intimacy and mutuality. Instead of receiving a blessing from a specially ordained man, the women present are likely to bless one another. They often share intensely personal experiences of God; they are not strangers to one another, as worshippers at a parish liturgy are apt to be. Women might bring to a feminist liturgy symbols that are meaningful to them or fashion symbols in the course of the liturgy that express their state of soul, their longings, their concern for peace and justice. And they well might not call any of this "feminist" at all. They simply find in this kind of prayer and worship a congenial setting where they can be themselves, speak in a language that is faithful to their experience of themselves and of the sacred, and find easier access to the God beyond gender. They also find a space in which they can preach God's Word without constraint.

Women's Preaching

The phrase "women's preaching" might appear to some as an oxymoron. Dr. Samuel Johnson, of course, compared a woman preaching to a dog standing on its hind legs: they don't do it well, but one is surprised that they can do it at all. One is *not* surprised by the smug sense of male superiority that informs this observation, however unwarranted it is, given the love, reverence and passion with which women have embraced God's word throughout history. The kind of prejudice that lies behind the remark of the 18th-century lexicographer, though, kept women out of pulpits in most Christian churches until well into the last century.

Today few would go so far as to characterize women's words as mere jabber and gibberish, but they may still look upon women's speech as unimportant and tangential to things that matter. For serious proclamation in the public realm, they may still look to men, and feel uneasy when a woman approaches a pulpit. But more and more women feel called to preach, and more and more people are welcoming their approach to preaching.

The New Testament handed down a mixed legacy in the matter of women's preaching and teaching. Jesus obviously did not consider preaching to be a male prerogative. It was to a Samaritan woman, an outsider and unlikely messenger, that he entrusted the revelation of his identity. It was she who brought to her people the message that she had encountered the Christ, and "they believed in him because of the woman's testimony." And we know that Jesus chose to commission women to announce the central mystery of our faith, the resurrection. Mary Magdalen, one of them, would later be called the "apostle to the apostles." Although kept in shadows in our tradition, women appear in the New Testament as leaders in the house churches, presbyters, preachers, prophets and teachers. Mary, Elizabeth, Anna, Mary Magdalen, Mary the mother of James, Junias, Prisca and Phoebe are mentioned by name, and Acts 21:9 makes mention of the four prophetic daughters of Philip. These latter, according to Eusebius, were so gifted ". . . that the provinces of Asia derive their apostolic origin from them."[30]

This unleashing of women's capacity to speak, proclaim and witness, this shared leadership of men and women in the Christ in whom "there is no male and female" was not destined to endure. More weight was given to the Pauline texts (I Cor 14:33a-35 and I Tm 2:11-15) prohibiting women from teaching or speaking in the assembly. Scripture scholars have demonstrated that these texts:

> . . . are pastoral injunctions in light of specific historical – cultural circumstances (including clear patriarchal bias) – not texts which were intended to be applied universally or handed down as "the Christian tradition."[31]

This fact did not prevent their being used to deny women official access to the preaching ministry in most Christian churches until relatively recently.

Mary Catherine Hilkert, in her article "Women Preaching the Gospel," (see note 31) briefly outlines the history of preaching. She traces the clericalization of ministry and the gradual restriction of preaching at the liturgy to the ordained. The hierarchical system placing women in subordination to men, laity to clergy, and clergy to bishop was well in place by the 7th century, and the law forbidding the laity, even unordained religious (and therefore all women), to preach was reiterated in the 1917 Code of Canon Law. It was the radical rethinking of church, priesthood and the prophetic mission that took place at Vatican II that opened the way for a rethinking of who should preach. The 1983 revision of Canon Law (Canon 766) states that laypersons can preach under certain circumstances, and various other documents that constitute church law have extended this possibility to the privileged form of preaching which is the homily during the liturgy. These little wedges have opened in response to many currents in the contemporary Catholic church: the recognition that official, authorized lay preaching exists in the tradition and that the roots of the preaching ministry are to be found in baptism; the demand for good preaching; the shortage of priests; the large corps of theologically literate religious and laypersons; the conviction that the entire assembly celebrates the liturgy and, therefore, the preaching function should not be the priest's alone; the critique of feminist scholars; and finally the realization that the Spirit blows where she will and ignores the niceties of human law when she distributes her gifts and charisms.

Having once attained the right to proclaim the Word of God (and in the Catholic church this right is still severely limited), do women bring anything unique to the art of preaching?

Christine Marie Smith, a United Methodist clergywoman, insists that they do. She is speaking particularly of preaching by women affected by feminist thought. In making her assertion, she tries to avoid the trap of stereotypical thinking which would dictate certain characteristics based on "natural" gender differences. Her conviction stems rather from her own personal, theological, and pastoral experience, and it is confirmed by 10 professors of homiletics whom she questioned. They singled out qualities such as the following:

- Women's sermons are better crafted than the sermons of men.

- Women are more creative and imaginative in dealing with the text; they have a high level of verbal skills and are excellent storytellers.

- They are inclusive in their language, images, and illustrations.

14 9They are relational and contextual in their preaching.

- Women use the imperative sparingly; they are invitational and address themselves to the whole person rather than simply to the mind of their hearers.

- Women tend to be more communal than men and to be more self-revelatory in their preaching.[3]2

All of the professors noted that the majority of preaching awards in recent years have gone to women. It is not surprising, then, that women are increasingly called upon to preach at weddings, religious professions, jubilees, re-treats and services of the Word. Women preachers have long since ceased to be an oddity at ecumenical gatherings and meetings, like the Call to Action and the Women's Ordination Conference. And women on pastoral teams in certain dioceses take their turn preaching at Sunday liturgies. In the tradition of Huldah, Deborah, Mary, Prisca and Junias, these women listen to the cries of the poor and the call of the spirit. From their position on the margin, they "witness to the new order, the communion in Christ, the liberating Gospel and the outpouring of the Spirit on all God's sons and daughters."[33] The whole church is richer for it.

Having found their voices, women are reshaping lan-guage and liturgy in ways that make their lives part of the ongoing story of redemption and salvation. If, in order to speak and pray authentically, they must congregate in all-women assemblies, they will continue to do that. But as they gain confidence in their own perspective on what it means to be sinful, as well as what it means to be whole, powerful, wise and compassionate, and as they experiment with different forms of prayer and worship, they will in-creasingly influence the entire church. We can permit ourselves to hope that the church's liturgy will eventually fully recognize and treasure real women, and not the women created from men's fears or men's romantic fancies. We can hope that our common prayer and worship will increasingly respect women's struggle for freedom, and the struggle of *all* who have been marginalized. As this process unfolds, liturgy will be revitalized and the church will become more truly itself.

Endnotes

1. See Dale Spender, *Man Made Language* (Boston: Routledge & Kegan Paul, 1980), 10-11.
2. See Barrie Thorne, Cheris Kramarae, and Nancy Henley, *Language, Gender and Society* (Rowley, Mass.: Newbury House Publishers, Inc., 1983), 8.
3. Nancy Henley, "This New Species that Seeks a New Language: On Sexism in Language and Language Change" in *Women and Language in Transition*, ed. Joyce Penfield (Albany: State University of New York Press, 1987), 4.
4. See Gail Ramshaw, *God Beyond Gender: Feminist Christian God Language* (Minneapolis: Fortress Press, 1995), 21.
5. Cheris Kramarae and others, eds., *Language and Power* (Beverly Hills: Sage Publications, 1984), 10.
6. Spender, 16.
7. Mary Stewart Van Leeuwen and others, *After Eden* (Grand Rapids, Mich.: W.B. Eerdmans, 1993), 357.
8. Spender, 43.
9. *On Lies, Secrets and Silence: Selected Prose, 1966-78* (New York: Norton, 1979), 204.
10. "The Transformation of Silence into Language and Action," A paper delivered to the Modern Language Association, Dec. 28, 1977, in *Sister Outsider* (Trumansburg, New York: Crossing Press, 1984), 41.
11. "The Rising Woman Consciousness in a Male Language Structure," *Andover Newton Quarterly* 12 (March 1972): 177-190.
12. Morton, 190.
13. See especially, *Webster's First New Intergalactic Wickedary of the English Language* (Boston: Beacon Press, 1987).

14. "Uses of the Erotic: The Erotic as Power," in *Sister Outsider*, 53.
15. A Passion for Friends: Toward a Philosophy of Female Affection (Boston: Beacon Press, 1986), 7-8.
16. See Victor Roland Gold and others, eds., *The New Testament and Psalms: An Inclusive Version* (New York: Oxford University Press, 1995).
17. Fiorenza, Elisabeth Schüssler, *In Memory of Her: A Feminist Theological Reconstruction of Christian Origins* (New York: Crossroad, 1990), 351.
18. See the *National Catholic Reporter*, 13 May 1994.
19. In Peter C. Finn and James M. Schellman, eds., *Shaping English Liturgy: Studies in Honor of Archbishop Denis Hurley* (Washington, D.C.: The Pastoral Press, 1990), 257-278.
20. See Henderson's assessment of ICEL's contribution, 278.
21. Anthony Lane, "Scripture Rescripted: In a New Version Bible Goes P.C.," *The New Yorker*, 2 Oct. 1995, 98.
22. *Worship: Renewal to Practice* (Washington, D.C.: The Pastoral Press, 1987), 215.
23. *In Her Own Rite: Constructing Feminist Liturgical Tradition* (Nashville: Abingdon Press, 1990), 86.
24. *Women and the Word* (N.Y.: Paulist Press, 1986), 26-27.
25. Henderson, 275.
26. *Ibid.*, 275.
27. *Ibid.*, 276.
28. "Principles of Feminist Liturgies," in *Women at Worship: Interpretations of North American Diversity*, eds. Marjorie Procter-Smith and Janet R. Walton (Louisville: Westminster/John Knox Press, 1993), 11.
29. See *Women-Church: Theology and Practice of Feminist Liturgical Communities* (San Francisco: Harper and Row, 1985), ch. 6.
30. Quoted in Elisabeth Schüssler Fiorenza, *In Memory of Her*, 299.
31. Mary Catherine Hilkert, "Women Preaching the Gospel," *Theological Digest* 33:4 (Winter 1986): 427-428.
32. Christine Marie Smith, *Weaving: A Metaphor and Method for Women's Preaching* (May, 1987), A Doctoral Dissertation presented to the Faculty of the Graduate School of Theology, Berkeley, California, 5-7.
33. Madonna Thelen, *A Threshold for the Spirit: A Feminist Model for Preaching* (December, 1990), A Master's Thesis presented to the Faculty of the Graduate Theological Union, 75.

Chapter 4

Women and Ministry

The juncture at which women and ministry meet in the 20th century is fraught with ambiguity. It's an exciting crossroad, full of possibility, but the women who meet there have serious questions to pose about the structures within which they live and work. They have questions about the nature of ministry, about power and authority, lay/clergy divisions, decision-making, leadership and ordination. Women's questions in these areas are not theirs alone. Increasing numbers of active, mainstream Catholics – male and female, lay and clerical – share these questions as they watch the contours of ministry adjust to the realities of the contemporary church.

The Evolution of Ministry

Not only in ours but in every age, the church's ministry was affected by the social, political and cultural milieu in which it was exercised, but until fairly recently we tended to forget this fact. For centuries Catholics and mainline Protestants equated ministry with ordained men, a full-time professional elite responsible for worship and sacrament, proclamation of the Word, administration, pastoral service, and oversight of the religious education of the laity. We came to imagine this arrangement as a God-given one, firmly rooted in the

Gospel. We have learned that, instead, it arose in response to changing historical circumstances.

In our own times, many factors have conspired to broaden, deepen and enrich our view of Christian service. Among Catholics, Vatican II opened out a new vision of church and of the place of the laity within it. In a renewed church, each baptized person was to understand her/himself as called to full discipleship, full participation in the mission of Jesus. The laity were called upon to share more actively in the liturgy and in parish life; they were encouraged to study theology. Significant numbers of women accepted these invitations. Women religious, largely concentrated in education and health care previously, began to diversify their ministries in response to the cries of the poor and the "signs of the times." Change was accelerated not only by the new ecclesiology, that found expression in the documents of Vatican II, but also by social currents: the women's movement, for instance, and the dramatic decline, at least in Europe and the United States, of candidates to the priesthood and to religious life.

Theologians like Yves Congar, Hans Küng, Elisabeth Schüssler Fiorenza, Thomas O'Meara, Edward Schillebeeckx, Rosemary Radford Ruether and Karl Rahner are among those who have placed the changing face of ministry in historical perspective. They have demonstrated that church, priesthood and ministry are not static realities put in place by Jesus in 1st-century Palestine. Ministry is, rather, a reality that has changed over time in response to new social conditions and to the irrepressible movement of the Spirit.

Despite the obvious differences between contemporary times and those of the early church, there is a resemblance between the expansion of ministry in our times and the profusion of gifts among the first followers of Jesus. Looking with fresh eyes at Scripture, we realize the extent to which active service to the Christian community was shared by the members of that community. Women and men alike were called to lead prayer, prophesy, teach, preach, heal and evangelize. Their call to service was rooted in their baptism; the form it took was in harmony with the gifts poured out upon them by a profligate Spirit. St. Paul is fond of listing the various gifts: wisdom, knowledge, administration, faith, healing, miraculous powers, the gift of tongues, interpretation of tongues, teaching, exhorting, the exercise of authority, giving of alms, doing the works of mercy – and, above all, love. The point of the abundance and diversity of gifts was to build up the body of Christ: "To each person the manifestation of the Spirit is given for the common good" (I Cor 12:7).

The place of women in the ministry of Jesus and in the 1st century of the Christian era has attracted a lot of attention in the past 25 years, both in the scholarly and the popular press. Those who would like to limit women's voice and role, as well as those who call for an extension of women's ministry in accord with their gifts, bolster their arguments with scriptural texts. Scripture has a way, however, of resisting attempts to force it neatly into any given ideological camp. There is general agreement, in any case, that women were full members of the early Christian community, that they were present when the Spirit was poured out at Pentecost, and that they were active in ministry. Elisabeth Schüssler Fiorenza writes:

> There is evidence that many of the functions which later were associated with the priestly ministry were in fact exercised by women, and no evidence that women were excluded from any of them. There were women instrumental in the founding of churches (Acts 18:2, 18f., I Cor 16:9, Rom 16:3f.); women with functions in public worship (I Cor 11:5); women engaged in teaching converts (Acts 18:26). Women prophets are attested (I Cor 11:5, Acts 21:9). In Paul's greeting

at the conclusion of *Romans* a woman minister (*diak-onos*) of the church at Cenchreae is named, and very likely a woman apostle (Junia-Rom 16:7). Thus while male leaders may have been more prominent and numerous in the early Church and while women's activities may have been somewhat limited by what was culturally permissible, many roles which ultimately were associated with the priestly ministry were evidently never restricted to men.[1]

What emerges from the Pauline communities is a picture of a revolutionary new equality of men and women "in the Lord," together with a recognition that the new creation had not yet been attained and that meanwhile certain social conventions were to be respected. Gifts were in plentiful supply, but they were to be used in a way that would build up the community. In Paul's day, that required some restraint in the way women's gifts were to be exercised, because the transcendence of boundaries in true Christian freedom could, in certain circumstances, give scandal. In our own day, what gives scandal is the fact that gender boundaries are being overcome more rapidly in society than in the church. Those who argue that church unity is compromised by the "woman question" are surely misguided. Can unity really be safeguarded by women's continued suppression? Isn't the *real* problem one of an outworn paradigm of domination?

The flexible, egalitarian, inclusive and charismatic model of ministry that characterized the fledgling church was not destined to endure. Thomas O'Meara charts ministry's "diminution" after the first generation of Christians. "Ministry shrinks," he writes, "ministry is institutionalized, ministry becomes priesthood and is grafted on to canonical posts from charismatic roots."[2] The functions of bishop (*episkopos*), presbyter or priest (*presbyteros*) and deacon (*diakonos*), which earlier had indicated ministries of leadership and service from which women were not necessarily and by definition excluded, gradually became precise offices.[3] The idea of a universal priesthood lost its vitality; the distinction between clergy and lay emerged and solidified; and power and authority in the church became more and more centralized in the hands of the ordained.

This progression was uneven, but it had already begun by the end of the 1st century, and was well-established everywhere by the 4th century. By this time Roman imperialism was affecting church organization and liturgy; bishops became officials of the Roman Empire; charisma became the province of the few; and the strong sense of community of the first Christians evolved into a more interior and individual piety. Worship moved out of the "house churches" and into splendid basilicas, and presiding at the Eucharist became the monopoly of bishop or priest. Rather than a proclamation of salvation, the worship service became a sacral mystery performed by a distant, cultic figure. At this time married clergy were apparently still the norm, but the regional Council of Carthage, held in 390, made a strong connection between ritual purity and ". . . the rule of continence and chastity."[4] By the time of the Gregorian Reform in the 11th century, lay people had been effectively removed from the liturgy, the intellectual life of the church, and leadership roles. Edward Schillebeeckx summarizes some of the effects of the growing "sacerdotalization" of the church:

> In the course of the centuries this gradual centralization of ministry at the expense of the baptism of the Spirit was to produce all kinds of side-effects. From it arose the pattern of (a) teaching (which is done by the church hierarchy), (b) explaining (which is done by the theologians), (c) listening to the teaching of the church – as explained by the theologians (which is done by the believers, called laity). This paradigm in fact makes believers subjectless. Vatican II already

contributed in some degree to the breakup of this ideological scheme.[5]

O'Meara highlights six key moments in the metamorphosis of ministry through the ages, moments in which he characterizes the typical minister as evangelist, bishop, priest, monk, *Herr Pastor* and curé. He avoids making judgments on any one of the periods, noting that ministry found a valid expression in each age, was shaped by the historical moment in which it evolved, and was a manifestation of the life of the Spirit in the church.[6] The lesson to be learned is simply this: there have been numerous models of organization and of ministry in the church, each with its richness and its limitations, and each responding to changing cultural and social circumstances. Each model survives in some form in today's church; none enjoys absolute pride of place or guaranteed survival into the future.

We are keenly aware that ministry continues to evolve as we approach the 21st century. Change seems to be accelerating and it does not occur without pain – whether for those who would like to stem its progress or for those who believe certain changes are long overdue.

Ministry Today

Liturgical, pastoral, and social ministry are no longer the sole preserve of the clergy or of religious. Since Vatican II we have witnessed what O'Meara terms an "explosion of ministry."

Significant lay participation in what used to be called the apostolate actually predates the Second Vatican Council, but in the last 25 years there has been an unmistakable shift in the types of ministry open to the laity, the level of education they bring to their ministries, and the number of lay women and men engaged in a wide variety of church roles. We have ceased to be surprised to receive communion from lay women and men, to hear them proclaim the Word, run RCIA programs, catechize, direct social justice projects, head up diocesan offices, edit diocesan papers, teach in seminaries, and enroll in theological study programs. The phenomenon of women, whether lay or religious, serving as pastors of parishes is still comparatively rare, but it is growing.

These changes are firmly rooted in the new ecclesiology that found expression in Vatican II documents. The latter, as well as subsequent official church documents, clearly indicate that there is a gospel discipleship that is common to all baptized Christians: lay and cleric, women and men, celibate and married, and people of every color and race. Their common discipleship makes equals of all of Christ's followers at this basic level, and it is fundamental to the very meaning of church and to the way the church is structured.[7] But the new ecclesiology is not interpreted in the same way by all, and its practical implications are not always understood. If understood, they are not always accepted or meaningfully applied. Furthermore, the weight of historical practice and of a lingering older theology of ordained priesthood combine to create tension in today's church around the issues of lay ministry, women's "role," and the possibility of women's ordination.

An address of John Paul II, given on July 2, 1993 to U.S. bishops gathered in Rome for their *ad limina* visits, reflects this tension. His topic was parishes, lay ministry and women.[8] In it he acknowledges that lay ministry is a positive development, and that the laity are active and responsible agents of the church's mission, but he fears that emphasis on baptismal equality will lead to minimizing the distinction between ordained and non-ordained. He turns attention once more to the role of the laity in sanctifying the secular realm – the domain of the earth, the world, and the human community – exhorting the bishops to remind the faithful that *this* is their "primary apostolate within the church." John Paul II grants that members of the laity can administer parishes in cases where there is a "temporary dearth of priests," but cautions that we must not "assume as normal . . . that a parish community be without a priest." And he underlines what he sees as an important distinction between women's human and civil rights (which the church must support) and their position in what concerns the "rights, duties, ministries and functions . . . within the church." In passing, he takes the opportunity to attack what he terms extreme forms of feminism, and to reiterate the church's interdiction on the ordination of women.

Obviously conscious of the growing discontent in the church with the unequal distribution of power and its not infrequent misuse, Pope John Paul II insists that the differences between men and women, clergy and lay, have nothing to do with "power understood in terms of privilege or dominion." The distinction of roles speaks rather to a relationship of complementarity, he says, not to one of superiority and inferiority. The arguments are familiar, but they are losing ground with those who operate out of a different anthropology and a different understanding of scripture, and with those who place a different emphasis on the teachings of Vatican II.

Mary Jo Weaver, for instance, challenges the notion of complementarity as expressed by the Pope, seeing in it a thinly disguised form of sex-role stereotyping. Complementarity assumes a permanent division of labor among women and men, based on their different "natures." The argument that their "difference" does not make women inferior prompts her to ask what inferiority means in the church. She turns to the anthropologist Sherry Ortner, who offers several types of evidence that constitute proof that a particular culture considers women inferior. Among them is this: ". . . social structural arrangements that exclude women for participation in or contact with some realm in which the highest powers of the society are felt to reside."[9] This observation applies equally well to ecclesial structures, and has obvious implications in the context of the Catholic church's continued restrictions on women's ordination and preaching.

In regard to the nature of lay ministry, the theologian Kenan Osborne offers a much more nuanced interpretation than John Paul II presents in his address. The role of the Christian, ordained or not, is an active ecclesial one. All who share in baptism, confirmation and eucharist participate in Jesus' mission of teaching/preaching (prophet), sanctifying (priest), and leading (king), and this truth should be reflected in church structures. Osborne states that the Christian's right and obligation to prophesy, sanctify and lead is exercised *primarily* within the church and *secondarily* within the sociopolitical arena. This is not a whimsical idea peculiar to Osborne; he points out that it is based on the documents of Vatican II (especially *Lumen Gentium*), the revised code of canon law and the church's ordinary magisterium.[10] Furthermore, it has become clear since Vatican II that the participation of all Christians in the mission and ministry of Jesus stems from their sacramental initiation and not from delegation by the hierarchy. Those who in pre-Vatican II days participated in the Catholic Action Movement will remember that their "lay apostolate" was presented as a sharing in the mission of the hierarchy. This view is no longer viable after Vatican II, but what remains a sticky theological problem, and one alluded to in John Paul's address, is just exactly how we are to understand the "essential" difference between the exercise of the priestly vocation by the ordained and the non-ordained. The official documents of Vatican II state the difference without explaining it. This intriguing question is not likely to fade away; it will occupy both theologians and those engaged in church ministry for the foreseeable future. So will the related question of women's participation in ministry.

Women's Ministry

We have already noted that women played a significant role among the disciples of Jesus, ministering with and to him during his lifetime, and subsequently proclaiming his life, death and resurrection. In the patristic period, women joined the desert fathers and, like them, became ascetics, teachers and counselors. In the 4th and 5th centuries, aristocratic women like Paula, Melania and Marcella of Rome founded monastic circles where they studied, prayed, healed and taught. And when, in the Middle Ages, monasteries became the source and standard of ministry, women no less than men gathered in them and found ample scope for their learning and holiness, and for their artistic and administrative gifts. Women mystics nourished the life of the church with their teaching, visions, poetry, leadership and pure grace.

In the modern period the Reformation and Counter-Reformation naturally affected the course of women's ministry. Protestants closed convents, removing this alternative to marriage and family from the lives of women of that tradition. They would subsequently find opportunities for teaching and evangelizing, principally in the more liberal Protestant traditions and in missionary work in the 19th century. In the Catholic tradition, women's ministry continued to be concentrated largely within convent walls.

To recognize that women have been a significant and luminous force in the furthering of God's realm throughout history must not lead us to imagine that they enjoyed the same education, freedom, autonomy or authority as men. It was the rare woman who attained the level of education available to men who were destined for ordination. The official church through much of its history, far from promoting higher education for nuns or for women in general, shared the common presumption that women were slow to understand, morally frail, and not to be trusted with public affairs. And if a few abbesses exercised the juridical powers of a bishop, women in the church were, in general, subject to legislation enacted by men.

In the case of religious, an effort to impose full cloister on all women who professed vows was begun in the late 13th century. They were to live behind high walls and to be seen and heard as little as possible. This did not entirely stop women from tending to the needs of the sick, poor and uneducated, however. Women religious in 19th century America, for instance, met the needs of wave after wave of European immigrants. In doing so, they experienced a new and exhilarating mobility and freedom.[11] The tension between women religious, who wanted to exercise an active apostolate, and church legislators, who wanted to impose upon them strict monastic closure and regulations, continued right up to the 20th century. The struggle for church recognition of women who wanted to work unimpeded in the thick of the intellectual and social conditions of their time was begun by Mary Ward in England in the 17th century, and was not won until 1877, when her congregation, the Institute of the Blessed Virgin Mary, was finally recognized as a religious community of active women religious.

The 1917 revision of canon law constituted a distinct setback for women religious. Restrictions were placed on the kind of work considered suitable for them, and their daily lives became subject to detailed regulation and to a deadening conformity. To enter religious life was to separate oneself from the world, making forays into it just long enough to carry on one's work of education or health care. This mentality ruled until the floodgates opened with Vatican II.

The Second Vatican Council called on women religious to suppress what was obsolete in their rules and constitutions, adapt what was valid, and introduce more participative forms of government. The Council's call for the Catholic church to read the signs of the times and to enter into solidarity with the world and the world's struggling peoples was not lost on women religious. In order better to answer this call, more and more sisters completed graduate study. They plunged into the liturgical and spiritual renewal given impetus by the Council, became active in civil rights movements, and initiated ministries to meet new social needs. And while some women religious may have been shaken in their identity by Vatican II's insistence that the call to holiness is universal, and that *every* Christian is called to participate actively in the mission and ministry of Jesus, most welcomed an equality in Christ that joined all Christians in their pursuit of God, truth, peace and justice. A growing consciousness of themselves precisely as women, and an ever-deeper involvement in the women's movement brought women religious into closer solidarity with all women and with the struggle for women's liberation from every oppression.

In the wake of Vatican II, women religious began to diversify their ministries. In addition to their work in education and health care, they entered into parish ministry, social work, social justice advocacy, community organizing, campus ministry, pastoral counseling, hospital chaplaincy, spiritual direction, retreat work, low-income housing, shelters for the homeless and for battered women, and work with persons with AIDS. At the same time, their numbers began to decrease dramatically, and lay men and women began to take their place in ministries traditionally associated with women religious: principals in Catholic grade schools and high schools, professors in Catholic colleges, administrators in Catholic hospitals.

Women's presence in American parish life has been an important factor in parish development since pioneer days.

Until Vatican II, however, it was confined mainly to the parish school, the Altar and Rosary Society, and various fund-raising efforts. Twenty years after Vatican II, the researchers who conducted the *Notre Dame Study of Catholic Parish Life* found laywomen and religious serving as lectors, eucharistic ministers, liturgical music directors, catechists, members of pastoral ministry teams, RCIA directors, and leaders of social concern programs. Well over half, and sometimes as high as 80 or 85% of those who lead adult Bible study, parish renewal programs and prayer groups are women. It is principally women who visit the sick and minister to the poor, the handicapped and the grieving.[12]

An interesting and discouraging observation of the Notre Dame Study, however, is that women's influence or power has not kept pace with their increased visibility and responsibility. While 58% of those, besides the pastor, who were named as leaders were women, women showed up in disproportionate numbers as being dissatisfied with parish decision-making. The study notes:

> The data hint that pastors and women in parish education have developed ways to share authority, but pastors and women organizing social activities, directing liturgical music, and leading social programs have not achieved a similar measure of shared respect and authority.[13]

It is no secret that job satisfaction is closely related to questions of power. Where power or influence does not match responsibility, the results, as sociologists have demonstrated, are defensiveness and low commitment. Patricia Wittberg, S.C., in a study of non-ordained workers in the Catholic church, found that a transfer of organizational power has not followed the trend of hiring laypersons, and this is especially the case when those persons are women.[14] Women religious, in particular, find that opportunities for meaningful participation in decision-making in parish work compare unfavorably with such opportunities in ministries sponsored by their congregations. Other sources of dissatisfaction among sisters and other lay workers as well are the ambiguity of function, overlapping roles, and lack of clarity in job titles. As in other areas of the work world, furthermore, positions sometimes diminish in status when held by women. Some parishes, of course, enjoy direction by parish teams in which true collaboration is evident among clergy and laity, women and men. These parishes are still not numerous enough.

Women as Pastors

In about 2% of Catholic parishes in the United States, non-ordained persons serve as parish administrators or "pastors." Most of them are women. They are concentrated in rural areas in the midwest, south, and western regions of the country. Ruth Wallace interviewed 20 of them in depth: eight married women with children, one single laywoman, and eleven women religious. They range in age from 33 to 67-years-old; 17 are Euro-American, three are Mexican-American. Wallace visited their parishes and interviewed parishioners and the priests who served the parishes as well.[15] The portrait that emerges of these pastors is one of women who are approachable, available, patient, warm, compassionate, down-to-earth, intelligent, understanding. Their style of leadership is collaborative, and they respect the parishioners' own authority. Women pastors tend to set up numerous committees, calling on the talents of many parishioners, and giving them the power to make key decisions. They offer training in lay leadership, and look upon their parishes as communities of Christians ministering to one another. Many parishes experienced growth within a year of the arrival of their woman pastor: more volunteers, more people on committees, more people at the Eucharist, more money in the collections, more spirit.

There are, of course, limits to the ministry women pastors can exercise. Liturgical and sacramental ministry, which is at the heart of a Catholic parish, is reserved to the ordained. The women interviewed by Wallace admitted to feelings of incompleteness and emptiness. After having done all the work of preparation, they often stand by and watch priests – who barely know the parishioners – baptize, anoint and witness marriages. One woman religious serving as spiritual leader of her parish expressed her frustration at, in effect, hearing confession and not being able to give absolution, blessing the sick and not being able to anoint them. A visiting priest presides at the Eucharist and may or may not welcome the presence of the woman pastor in the sanctuary; he may or may not authorize her to preach. One woman used the analogy of being asked to dig without tools, or being told, "The tools are there, but you cannot touch them." Yet some of the women hesitate to say that the ordination of women is the answer. Much of their effectiveness seems related to the fact that they are laypersons untouched by clerical culture.

The experience of the women in Wallace's study, women who administer and serve as spiritual leaders of parishes, is illustrative of the opportunities and constraints facing many women in ministry in the Catholic church. They are happy and effective in their work, but their limited authority and empowerment frustrates them and often the people they serve. What one bishop or visiting priest permits, supports and encourages may be withdrawn by his successor. A male parishioner interviewed by Wallace expressed his concern about the inequities and obstacles facing women in ministry:

> I think that whoever came up with this pastoral administrator job for the religious [women] and lay people should get into a position in our church that they would enlighten the view of our upper-echelon

people. We have to do something. We are committing suicide. We just have to change. I feel we are wasting an awful lot of our resources. We should have ordination of women. It is just puzzling to me that we don't. People have to be protecting their own turf.[17]

Women and the Priesthood

It is doubtful that the latest Vatican pronouncement on women's ordination did anything to relieve this man's puzzlement. The statement, issued on October 28, 1995 by the Congregation for the Doctrine of the Faith, and signed by Joseph Cardinal Ratzinger, came in the form of a *Responsum ad Dubium,* a response to a question. The question was "Whether the teaching that the Church has no authority whatsoever to confer priestly ordination on women, which is presented in the Apostolic Letter *Ordinatio Sacerdotalis,* is to be held definitively, is to be understood as belonging to the deposit of faith." The answer was "in the affirmative." The response elaborates briefly:

> This teaching requires definitive assent, since, founded on the written word of God, and from the beginning constantly preserved and applied in the Tradition of the Church, it has been set forth infallibly by the ordinary and universal Magisterium (cf. Second Vatican Council, *Dogmatic Constitution on the Church, Lumen Gentium* 25, 2). Thus, in the present circumstances, the Roman Pontiff, exercising his proper office of confirming the brethren (cf. Lk 22:32), has handed on this same teaching by a formal declaration, explicitly stating what is to be held always, everywhere, and by all, as belonging to the deposit of faith.

This pronouncement, which stunned, saddened and enraged countless Catholics, has not buried the question of women's ordination, but *has* turned the spotlight on the meaning of infallibility and on the appropriate use (if any) of this papal prerogative. Those accustomed to reading Vatican documents and measuring their weight agree that this type of "infallible" statement is the weakest kind, not having been delivered *ex cathedra*, that is, from the chair of Peter.

The *Responsum ad Dubium* nevertheless declares that the ban on women's ordination is an infallible part of Church teaching and tradition. Many respectable scholars, however, insist that a male-only priesthood is a matter of church order or discipline and, as such, cannot be made a matter of faith, much less an infallible teaching. Nicholas Lash, a professor of divinity at Cambridge, wrote in the Dec. 2, 1995 issue of *Tablet*, that the attempt of Cardinal Ratzinger, or of the Pope, to *make* a teaching to be founded on the Word of God or to be part of the tradition of the Church simply by asserting that it is, does not make it so. He concludes the article by saying:

> The attempt to use the doctrine of infallibility, a doctrine intended to indicate the grounds and character of Catholic confidence in official teaching, as a blunt instrument to prevent the ripening of a question in the Catholic mind, is a quite scandalous abuse of power, the most likely consequence of which will be further to undermine the very authority which the Pope seeks to sustain.

Despite this attempt, the question has, indeed, been ripening in the Catholic mind, and has gained steadily increasing support since the 1970s when the debate began in earnest. By 1976, with the vote of the Episcopalian church to ordain women, all of the mainline Protestant churches had accepted women for ordination. The decision of the Episcopalian church was significant since they, like the Roman Catholic church, see in the priest a representative of Christ. Rome moved quickly, too quickly in the mind of many, to make a statement even before there was theological clarity or consensus on the question. Paul VI's response, entitled *Declaration on the Question of the Admission of Women to the Ministerial Priesthood* (*Inter Insigniores*), came in 1976 on the heels of the vote by the Episcopal church and of the first Women's Ordination Conference, held in Detroit in 1975. The *Declaration* introduced a new argument into the debate. The old one, based on the notion that the order of creation entails the headship of man and the subordination of woman (or man's superiority and women's inferiority), having been generally discredited, a new one was proposed. No more palatable, it claimed that although equal to men in dignity, women do not bear a natural resemblance to Christ and so cannot represent him sacramentally. A further argument centered on the will of Christ, who might have but, in fact, did not choose women to be among the Twelve.

Theologians, historians and scripture scholars were quick to point out the weakness of these arguments. Since the real significance of the Incarnation is that Christ became *human*, what is to prevent women's representing him? If the priest represents God, who is neither male nor female, why cannot women made in God's image represent God? If the priesthood represents church, then the ordination of both women and men would be appropriate, and can even be deemed necessary if the church is to be represented in its fullness. As for the 12 male apostles, this argument equates apostolic ministry with ordained ministry, a conflation that is not warranted by scripture.

Scholars accepted the *Declaration* as a statement that was authoritative but not definitive. Pointing out that through a *Commentary* Rome called explicitly for further theological debate, they obligingly produced a rich body of reflection on the nature and meaning of priesthood, its historical development, and the cultural influences that have shaped it. Meanwhile, the pastoral service of women in parishes was convincing more and more of the people in the pews that women's continued exclusion from ordination was unhealthy and unjust. They recognized the "priestly" presence of women in their service: their theological training, their compassion, their skill in listening, their ability to engage parishioners in prayer and worship, spiritual renewal and action for justice.

Because the debate, far from retreating into the shadows, threatened, on the contrary, to become ever more intense, Pope John Paul II in 1994 made it clear in another statement, entitled *Ordinatio Sacerdotalis,* that the ban on women's priesthood was a "definitive" teaching of the church. He forbade further discussion of it, but the debate continued undiminished. This is what provoked the 1995 statement that introduced the dreaded word "infallible" into the discussion. The infallibility in question is that of the ordinary and universal magisterium. That is, the exclusion of women from ordained priesthood is based on the assumption that bishops around the world hold this exclusion to be part of the deposit of faith. There is ample evidence that this is not the case, however, and so we await the last word on whether or not this teaching is infallible in the technical sense of the term. Meanwhile the millions of Catholics who disagree with the pronouncement have continued to question the logic and the justice of acknowledging women's full equality and personhood and denying them one of its sacraments. The Catholic Theological Society of America, at its June 1996 meeting, drafted a position paper designed to stimulate further study and discussion of the issue by theologians and theological faculties. And in November 1996, the Call to Action and Future Church launched a major dialogue on the priest shortage crisis and the availability for ordination of women and married men. The conference provided a forum for a discussion of the scriptural, theological, canonical and pastoral issues involved in the church's present policies on ordination.

Current questions surrounding ordination go well beyond the issues of ordaining women and married men, however. As early as the mid-70s, shortly after the Women's Ordination Conference was launched, some women began to question the wisdom of seeking entrance into clerical ranks. Harboring a deep suspicion of the rigid hierarchies that mark orders, and the church structures built on them, many women, and notably Elisabeth Schüssler Fiorenza, warned against women's being diverted from their own concerns to support privileged models of leadership that have little to do with the gospel ideal of a "discipleship of equals." Those women who continued to seek a change in church policy in regard to women's ordination recognized early the need to work simultaneously for a transformed priesthood. The tension that existed in bud in the 1970s surfaced full-blown at the Women's Ordination Conference held in Arlington, Virginia in November 1995. Those who continue to advocate the ordination of women embrace the vision of a discipleship of equals, but are not convinced that it is incompatible with the ordination of women to a renewed priestly ministry. Those who have come to hold that feminist goals and the nature of Catholic priesthood are irreconcilable believe that women's energy should be spent on creating a different kind of ministry in a different kind of church.

Mary Hunt, a Catholic theologian who is in full sympathy with those who have lost patience with the patriarchal trappings of the church, points out, nevertheless, that feminists, with reason, celebrated the consecration of Bishop Barbara Harris as the first woman bishop in the Episcopal church. She proposes that:

> The challenge for the women-church movement is to
> let neither the anti-ordination position nor the pro-

ordination position predominate, but to let the positions co-exist in mutual critique.[18]

The presence of women in publicly recognized positions of authority and power is clearly one of the issues that, whether or not it is made explicit, lies at the heart of the debate. The public/private dichotomy resurfaces here, with the stubborn notion that men belong properly in the first arena and women in the second. While applauding the "legitimate" gains of the feminist movement, Pope John Paul II keeps insisting on women's special nature, which fits her best for marriage and family. In a message delivered to a general audience in December 1995, he chided women who want to be "copies of men." It is difficult for him to imagine that women want to work for any other reason than to provide for the needs of a family. That work and achievement and public voice might have something to do with women's selfhood, just as they do for men, seems not to occur to him.

We must acknowledge, however, that feminists themselves are ambiguous about the power issue. Carolyn G. Heilbrun writes:

> Although feminists early discovered that the private is the public, women's exercise of power and control, and the admission and expression of anger necessary to that exercise, has until recently been declared unacceptable.[19]

Her opinion is borne out by the fact that women often proclaim themselves sad about pronouncements about women and women's ordination that originate in the Vatican, but seldom angry or enraged. The Leadership Conference of Women Religious, for instance, declared themselves grieved, concerned and puzzled in regard to the *Responsum ad Dubium*. These sentiments are acceptable ones for women. The leaders of women religious apparently accepted the "definitive" nature of the ban on women's ordination, but challenged the church to find other ways, then, to share decision-making power with non-ordained members of the church.

We have few models in church or society for the proper understanding and use of power. Heilbrun writes:

> The true representation of power is not of a big man beating a smaller man or a woman. Power is the ability to take one's place in whatever discourse is essential to action and the right to have one's part matter. This is true in the Pentagon, in marriage, in friendship, and in politics.[20]

We will return to the question of power and leadership in the next chapter. Meanwhile, it is interesting to note that the principal books on ordained ministry, which has been the locus of power in the church, are by men. Women's voices have been missing from the discourse because women have been barred from the experience of sacramental ministry. Catherine Mowry Lacugna observes:

> Both professional theology and professional ministry have been enriched and transformed by the presence of women, while the presbyteral office has not been. A case in point would be "theology of ministry." Even though many women have pastoral experience, because it is not presbyteral or strictly speaking "sacramental" they are prohibited from reflecting theologically on presbyteral ministry "from within."[21]

While appreciating the work of ordained ministers on ordained ministry (and lay ministry), we can only imagine how women's personal experience and theological reflection on this aspect of church life would enrich and very likely revolutionize the institution. The questions posed by Elisabeth Schüssler Fiorenza at the 1995 Women's Ordination Conference, however, implied that women seeking ordination were not interested in revolution. She asked quite pointedly:

> What is the dream that still needs to be realized? Is it
> that women in the Roman Catholic church finally will
> be able to call themselves "Reverend," to wear the
> clerical collar, to don clerical vestments or to receive
> clerical privileges, to receive the indelible mark of
> essential difference, the promotion to upper-class
> status, not only in the church but also in heaven? Is
> it a dream to eat a piece of the clerical pie, even if
> we choke on it . . . ?[22]

These questions seem judgmental and unfair. Isn't it
possible, even probable, that the women whose jobs place
them in a position to exercise a sacramental ministry would
like simply to be able to offer the comfort and grace that
sacraments afford to those whom they have prepared for
those sacraments? The association of ordination and privilege, clericalism and the abusive exercise of authority surely
repels them as much as it repels any authentic disciple of
Christ. Isn't it, rather, the association of ordination and public
recognition of a call and of certain gifts, ordination and the
power to influence decisions, ordination and service that
attracts them? Still, we must concede that exclusion from
complete absorption into certain forms of institutional
power, in this case the priesthood, has its advantages. It
leaves more space for critical reflection and for challenge
to that power and to the distinctions and barriers that it
perpetuates.

The questions surrounding ordination are admittedly
complex. One idea that deserves further attention is that of
extending ordination. Thomas O'Meara suggests that we
look upon ordination not as a liturgical exercise of episcopal
power, not as something bestowed by juridical decree, but
as a ". . . communal liturgy of public commissioning to a
specific ministry."[23] These ministries might include liturgical
and sacramental service, governance, administration, preaching, teaching, healing, action for justice, and new ministries

that gain importance and permanence in the eyes of national or local churches. Can we envision a church in which *all* ministries would be open to *all* who have the gifts and the necessary preparation to exercise them? And can we hope someday to arrive at a theology of ministry in which distinctions such as lay ministry and clerical ministry, ordained and non-ordained ministry, will be meaningless? Meanwhile we must push at the boundaries which may once have been valid and useful, but which now restrict the full unfolding of God's realm.

Ministry to Women

Evolving social realities and a changed consciousness among women have made it necessary for those who minister to them to develop new modes of pastoral care. The women's movement has provided new frameworks for interpreting women's experience and women's life cycle; it has redefined gender expectations, if not the very notion of gender itself. Ministers, women and men alike, who are not sufficiently aware of the issues that concern women or who are incapable of seeing these issues through the eyes of women will obviously be unable to respond to them effectively.

Pastors and their associates, pastoral counselors, spiritual directors and hospital chaplains are called upon today to minister to women who are struggling with feelings of guilt and anger as they reread and reinterpret the text of their lives. As women seek to balance their need for self-direction and autonomy with their need for mutuality and relationship, and as they move away from reliance on outside authority figures and toward confidence in their own internal authority, they need a new kind of direction, a new kind of listening. The words and approach of anyone operating out of old paradigms or dated stereotypes are doomed to harm or offend women who are carving out new identities, often while simultaneously dealing with painful social realities.

Divorced women and other single mothers struggling to support children, women suffering from the effects of domestic violence, women juggling the obligations of work and home, women faced with the care of aging parents just as they are relieved of child care, are not in a state of mind to hear of the sanctifying effects of suffering and hardship and the merits of the work ethic. Lesbian women do not need counseling based on the conviction that their sexual orientation is ordered toward an intrinsic moral evil. Pregnant women and menopausal women will not find life-giving words from counselors who look upon women's bodies and reproductive cycles as mysterious at best or evil at worst, or as liabilities or illnesses to be suffered as best one can. Women dealing with infertility or miscarriage or mastectomies do not want to hear these realities minimized or met with embarrassed silence. Young women who are educated and called to ministry in the church, but who are frustrated by church teaching and church practice, are not likely to heed advice to submit graciously to regulations that inhibit the full exercise of their gifts. Women searching for new forms of prayer and worship do not need to be shunned as annoying complainers or dangerous heretics.

What these and all women seeking comfort and direction from church representatives do need are attentive listening and responses that indicate familiarity with the deeper implications of women's raised consciousness and of the new horizons opened out by feminist theology, ethics, and spirituality. They need ministers who have insight into the stereotypes surrounding gender, class, race, age, sexual orientation and physical limitations that are at the root of so much suffering. They need ministers who will respect their experience, honor their strength, understand their feelings and help them integrate all of this with their faith.

Platitudes, facile reassurances, swift and easy judgments, and condescending advice will fall very wide of the mark. Women need and deserve, rather, preachers, spiritual companions and counselors who will provide a theological context and church environment that keeps pace with the changing realities of their self-identity and their lives.

Feminist Ministry

In the field of ministry, as in virtually every field, feminists for the past decade have been articulating a vision and creating new models of service. The themes of relationship, mutuality, inclusiveness, shared authority, justice, and salvation as embodied love resurface here in the context of action and service in God's household.

Feminists count themselves among those who refuse to equate Christian call and vocation with ordained ministry. As ministers themselves, they see their role as one of encouraging everyone to claim their ministerial privilege and responsibility, to participate in the common ministry of the community according to the gifts they have received in the Spirit. They resist placing these gifts in hierarchical order, seeing each of them rather as Paul did, that is, as essential elements in the building of community. One feminist in Christian ministry expresses her growing awareness of the collective character of ministry:

> Not only do we recognize that, however important the specific work of isolated individuals, most of us can work effectively over a long period only when that work is undertaken with the support and shared effect of others having similar concerns. The longer I remain in this parish, the less I am preoccupied with "mobilizing" others and the more I am committed to participating in a common struggle rooted in an identifiable community of people.[24]

The common struggle encompasses the effort to establish right relationships – with God, self, other and the living universe. It involves the skills to analyze and change unjust power arrangements in the home, the local church, the universal church, and in society at large. It suggests a capacity to see in difference an opportunity for growth and a force for change. The common struggle finds nourishment in meaningful prayer, worship and celebration, and in a spirituality shot through with a sense of the political as well as a sense of the sacred.

Feminist ministers are conscious of the interrelations that connect every form of oppression, and are in solidarity with all who seek justice. They are especially sensitive to approaches to theology and spirituality that harm women, and they are committed to honoring women's experience and encouraging them to speak their own language of God. Recognizing that ". . . women have lacked the power and freedom to participate fully in recording, governing, and interpreting the life of faith communities,"[25] they are determined to right the balance and enrich the life of the church by assuring women's full participation in every aspect of it.

It is clear that the questions posed at the beginning of this chapter about the nature of ministry, power and authority, lay/clergy divisions, leadership and ordination are far from being resolved. It is equally clear that women will have more and more voice and influence in the continuing dialogue.

Endnotes

1. "Women and Priestly Ministry: The New Testament Evidence," *CSR Bulletin* 11:2 (1980): 45; quoted in Thomas Franklin O'Meara, O.P., *Theology of Ministry,* (New York: Paulist Press, 1983), 84-85.

2. O'Meara, 79.

3. Both Raymond Brown and Elisabeth Schüssler Fiorenza conclude that in the first Christian communities, ministry and leadership depended not on age or gender, but on one's spiritual gifts. Brown,

for instance, cites I Timothy 5:1 as follows: "Do not rebuke an older man/presbyter *(presbuteros)* but admonish him as one would a father, younger men/deacons *(neoteroi)* as brothers, older women/ presbyters *(presbuterai)* as mothers, younger women/deacons (*neoterai*) as sisters in all propriety." In R.E. Brown, "Episkope and episkopos: The New Testament Evidence," *Theological Studies* 41 (1980): 335.

4.   See Michael Crosby, *Celibacy: Means of Control or Mandate of the Heart?* (Notre Dame: Ave Maria Press, 1995), 45.

5.   *The Church with a Human Face: A New and Expanded Theology of Ministry* (New York: Crossroad, 1985), 122. For a learned and exhaustive study of the evolution of the status of the laity in the church see Kenan B. Osborne, OFM, *Ministry: Lay Ministry in the Roman Catholic Church, Its History and Theology* (New York: Paulist Press, 1993).

6.   O'Meara, ch. 5.

7.   See Kenan B. Osborne's *Ministry,* ch. 12 for a detailed discussion of the implications of a common gospel discipleship.

8.   Origins 23 (15 July 1993): 124-126.

9.   New Catholic Women (San Francisco: Harper and Row, 1985), 52.

10.   Osborne, 539-540.´

11.   See Mary Ewens, O.P., "Removing the Veil: The Liberated American Nun," in *Women of Spirit: Female Leadership in the Jewish and Christian Traditions,* eds. Rosemary Radford Ruether and Eleanor McLaughlin (New York: Simon and Schuster, 1979), ch. 9. This volume gives excellent snapshots of women of various religious traditions throughout history, acting, speaking, and shaping their traditions in spite of the limitations placed upon them.

12.   David C. Leege and Joseph Gremillion, eds., *Notre Dame Study of Catholic Parish Life* (University of Notre Dame Press, 1984-1987).

13.   Report #9, December 1986.

14.   See "Non-Ordained Workers in the Catholic Church: Power and Mobility among American Nuns," *Journal for the Scientific Study of Religion* 28 (June 1989): 148-161.

15.   See her analysis of the data in *They Call Her Pastor: A New Role for Catholic Women* (Albany, N.Y.: Suny Press, 1992).

16.   *Ibid.,* 143.

17.   *Ibid.,* 175.

18.   "The Challenge of 'Both-And' Theology," in *Women and Church: The Challenge of Ecumenical Solidarity in an Age of Alienation,* ed. Melanie A. May (New York: Friendship Press, 1991), 30.

19.   *Writing a Woman's Life* (New York: Ballantine Books, 1988), 17.

20.   *Ibid.,* 18.

21. "Catholic Women as Ministers and Theologians," *America*, 10 October 1992, 238-248.
22. *National Catholic Reporter,* 1 December 1995, 9.
23. O'Meara, 198.
24. Lynn N. Rhodes, *Co-Creating: A Feminist Vision of Ministry* (Philadelphia: Westminster Press, 1987), 119-120.
25. *Ibid.,* 26.

Chapter 5

Women and Leadership

The idea of women as leaders is less foreign to us than to previous generations, but even now the notion strikes some as faintly incongruous or unseemly. It strikes terror in others.

Women who seek leadership positions in business, in the professions or in the church still find considerable resistance; indeed, they may be subtly punished for moving outside role requirements that situate women far from all that is powerful or prestigious. This is especially true in areas not traditionally associated with their interests or skills. While they make headway more easily in fashion, health care or teaching (and even here men enjoy greater access to top executive levels), they run into strong and sometimes insuperable barriers if they set their sights on influential levels of leadership in large corporations, the government, politics, higher education or the church. Women are grossly underrepresented in senior leadership positions in these areas; the glass ceiling and the stained glass ceiling remain firmly in place. In areas such as police and fire departments, construction, engineering or the military, women are striving not so much to attain leadership positions as to gain respectable footholds in the field.

Added to the obstacles imposed from without are the uneasiness and doubts that arise within women themselves.

They do not easily shed the effects of centuries of conditioning that have steered them into subordinate, secondary and supportive roles. They wonder if, in assuming the kind of authority and power traditionally associated with men, women risk losing the ability or desire to offer the kind of loving, nurturing care commonly associated with women. And, women ask themselves, doesn't the world, at this juncture, need more rather than less of these qualities? Their self-doubt is reinforced by men whose self-interest lies in maintaining the traditional arrangements in which women listen and serve, while men lead and control.

Women, furthermore, have relatively few models to guide them in their exercise of power and leadership. Determined to leave the helpless, little-girl image behind, they nevertheless are repelled by the overt, rigid, insensitive, authoritarian style of leadership they have experienced at the hands of some men. Neither does the kind of indirect, wheedling, manipulative power associated with those habitually excluded from centers of command and influence hold any appeal for them. They are searching for ways to lead that are decisive and direct, but not overbearing; they are seeking to eliminate from the notions of power and authority the aura of domination and coercion. Certain trends in the contemporary world favor this effort. But it remains true that the road to wide and effective leadership by women is blocked by strong and stubborn cultural, religious, psychological and sociological factors. Let's consider some of them.

Gender, Power, and Authority

Leadership is intimately bound up with issues of power and authority, and gender plays a central role in the web that connects all three. In the first place, and most obviously, power, mastery and control are attributes that conventional wisdom assigns to men, while respectful submission, care and nurturance characterize the ideal woman. Just as women's silence completes men's speech, so their compliance complements men's authority. The familiar dichotomies emerge once again: woman is the embodiment of all that is earthy and dangerous, man is the essence of rational composure; woman is fanciful and weak-willed, man is emotionally and morally strong. Furthermore, woman's natural gifts and tendencies, her obligations as wife and mother, destine her to operate in the private sphere; man's greater emotional stability, analytic power, and ambition fit him to play an active role in the world of affairs. The realities of the contemporary world – the gradual blurring of gender roles, for instance, and women's unprecedented entrance into the workplace rob these stereotypic expectations of their force, but they still haunt Western consciousness and affect relations between the sexes in both the personal and public spheres. Masculine rule is too firmly embedded in our language, in our symbols and rituals, and in our thought processes to yield easily to the challenges that are only beginning to confront it.

Margaret Atwood gives a deft little sketch of how gender power arrangements and some attendant binary oppositions work out in literature:

> Men favor heroes who are tough and hard: tough with men, hard with women. Sometimes the hero goes soft on a woman but this is always a mistake. Women do not favor heroines who are tough and hard. Instead they have to be tough and soft . . . . Men's novels are about how to get power. Killing and so on, or winning and so on. So are women's novels, though the method is different. In men's novels, getting the woman or women goes along with getting the power. It's a perk, not a means. In women's novels you get the power by getting the man. The man is the power.[1]

It will take courageous leaps of imagination to forge new categories of perception, and thereby transcend a system that has been taken for granted for so long. Those who attempt it must face a multitude of poets and philosophers, theologians, psychologists, storytellers and filmmakers who have reinforced the power arrangements that continue to blind us to humanizing alternatives.

Women themselves have tended to accept a system of male domination that appears to be universal, and so needs no justification. Excluded from the circles where meaning and boundaries are defined, women have not been in a position to question what they were told about themselves by those who discounted female experience and conceived of themselves as the earth's natural rulers. The one area where women's power cannot be denied or countermanded, their reign over infant children, serves only to justify adult male dominion later. Having been totally dependent on female rule as children, men spend the rest of their lives controlling and harnessing the power of women. Adult women themselves turn to male authority as a refuge from the unilateral power their mothers exercised over them as infants. Dorothy Dinnerstein dissects this interplay of female and male power with uncommon psychological insight in her book *The Mermaid and the Minotaur: Sexual Arrangements and Human Malaise.* She exposes the unhealthy symbiosis whereby men shape the world through their exercise of overt, formal power, and women play the role of domesticated critic, a kind of court jester ". . . willingly ruled by the power she mocks."[2] We have reached a point, though, where women are less and less willing to play this game.

Feminists rejected the rules some time ago. And many, both women and men, have come to see that the split between male and female spheres of influence, between male and female sensibilities, threatens to poison personal relationships, and beyond that, to further dehumanize the worlds of business and politics. The old bargains – I must be dumb so he can be smart; weak so he can be strong; silent so he can speak; obedient so he can command – prosper neither the human race nor, ultimately, the planet we inhabit. The first step in renegotiating the bargain, or better still, in scrapping it entirely in favor of a system of self-creative humanness for all, consists in women's becoming the authors of their own lives.

Women, Self-Creation, and Authority

The words authority, author and authentic are closely related, as Warren Bennis points out in his book on leadership. This work is focused largely on men, but he acknowledges that there is evidence that ". . . women, too, are happier when they have invented themselves, instead of accepting without question the roles they were brought up to play." He continues:

> I cannot stress too much the need for self-invention. To be authentic is literally to be your own author . . . to discover your own native energies and desires, and then to find your own way of acting on them. When you've done that, you are not existing simply in order to live up to an image posited by the culture or some other authority or by a family tradition. When you write your own life, then no matter what happens, you have played the game that was natural for you to play.[3]

What Bennis fails to acknowledge is that the roles men are brought up to play encourage them in the direction of quest, adventure and self-invention. Men are expected to write their own lives; women are expected to follow the script written by a patriarchal culture. When they deviate from it, they are plagued by feelings of guilt and abnormality.

Carolyn Heilbrun, in her *Writing a Woman's Life* documents the struggles of women whose energies and sense of possibilities led them to reject the scripts handed to them. Experiencing the need for power, knowledge and the right to speak with authority, some women assumed men's names or men's dress. Willa Cather, for instance, became William Cather in college, and dressed like a man in her attempt to create a life for herself and to overcome what she experienced as gender barriers to her ambition. Dorothy Sayers, in response to men who found women in men's dress an unbecoming spectacle, is quoted as saying, "If the trousers do not attract you, so much the worse; for the moment I do not want to attract you. I want to enjoy myself as a human being."[4] Enjoying herself as a human being meant for Margaret Fuller finding some outlet for the power, generosity and tenderness she experienced within herself. This combination of traits was not one that society was accustomed to find in a single person, however, and Fuller at 21 saw few avenues for channelling her energy and her gifts in ways that would, at the same time, satisfy her and serve humanity.

Some doors have been opened since but, as Heilbrun sees it, the challenge now is to ". . . stop inscribing male words, and rewrite our ideas about . . . a female impulse to power, as opposed to the erotic impulse which alone is supposed to impel women."[5] This will involve a continuing bid for public power, and the exercise by women of their right to participate in the discourse that leads to action in all of the realms that affect human life and development: church, state, business, family and politics. Feminist biographers are now uncovering texts that reflect their subjects' struggles and ambitions in the public sphere, although their previously published biographies and even their autobiographies present them as intuitive, domestic and passive. The literal rewriting of women's lives, the bringing to light of their desire to achieve, their experience of their bodily selves, their bonds with other women – all that previously had been ignored or hidden – provides women today with narratives, plots and examples that strengthen their determination to create themselves and to define a female culture. In that newly defined culture women claim their power and their place in the public domain. In this regard, Audre Lorde issues an invitation:

> I ask each of you to sit for a minute, reach deep inside of you, and feel what it means to be a citizen of the most powerful country in the world. For those of us who are Black, it is not enough to say, "I'm Black – I do not have a part of that power." For those of us who are women, it is not enough to say, "I am a woman – I stand outside that power." Each one of us is responsible. That responsibility and that power are relative, but they are real. And if I do not identify that power within myself, if you do not identify it within yourselves – own it, learn to use it for the future – it will be used against you and me and our children and the world.[6]

Church Authority and Women

Women in their relationship to the church and its authority have not, of course, been untouched by the movements impelling women toward self-definition, self-creation, authoritative speech and positions of leadership. Women religious, for instance, in the wake of Vatican Council II, and with the encouragement of church officials, began a process of renewal which awakened in them a strong sense of their identity as women and as responsible moral agents and decision-makers. Focused at first on externals, such as dress and schedule, the process quickly moved into questions of identity, ministry and governance, and brought women religious far beyond what church authorities had envisioned. The latter had not foreseen the length and depth of the transformation of religious life and ministry that followed upon the appropriation, especially by American religious, of their own experience and of their legitimate personal and congregational authority.

The movement of American women religious from positions of dependence and docile compliance, with norms defined by others, to the kind of autonomy and rightful use of power that characterizes healthy adults, brought them into inevitable conflict with Rome. *The Transformation of American Catholic Sisters*, by Lora Ann Quiñonez and Mary Daniel Turner, chronicles defining moments in the struggle. One of these moments was the long process required to rewrite the constitutions of religious congregations. Women religious participated fully within their own communities in reshaping their identity in the light of the Gospel, their founding inspiration and their contemporary experience. When congregation leaders presented the revised constitutions to Roman authorities for approval, areas of crucial importance to their membership often met with incomprehension and resistance. Sticking points centered on questions of the interpretation of obedience, whether to religious superiors or to the Pope, the right to participate in decisions that affected the life of the institution and of the individuals within it, religious dress and residence. In the negotiations that led to final approval, religious leaders often felt their rights had been abridged or ignored, and lamented the lack or limits of legal recourse. They and the members of their congregations had come to see as essential the kind of autonomy that means being accountable for one's own action. Gradually through resistance, dialogue and compromise in terms of language, if not principle, congregations won approval of their reconceived and rewritten constitutions, and in the process succeeded in realigning themselves in relation to church authorities. The whole experience raised the question in many American congregations of the value of canonical status, and of the need to win the approval of men of another mindset and culture for the documents that embody the traditions and values that rule their lives.

There are numerous other examples of the clash that occurs between ecclesiastical authorities and women whose actions betray a desire for change in regard to the church's treatment of women, or a desire to take control over their own lives. They give evidence of how deeply the autonomous existence of women threatens the celibate, clerical power system. Questions involving sexuality and reproduction are especially sensitive ones, a fact brought home with force to the signers of the *New York Times* ad stating that a diversity of opinion existed in the Catholic Church in regard to abortion, and calling for dialogue on the question. The ad, which appeared in the October 7, 1984 issue of the newspaper, was a reaction to the pressure being brought against Geraldine Ferraro and other Catholic political figures for their position of pro-choice. Together with hundreds of lay people, 24 women religious had signed the ad. Perhaps because of their position as public witnesses to church teaching, and because they were easier to target than the lay signers, the women religious were subjected to interrogation by highly-placed ecclesiastical authorities, and threatened with expulsion from their religious communities. They were asked to sign statements indicating their adherence to Roman Catholic teaching on abortion. Many felt that the statements they signed or the statements presented to Rome by their religious superiors did not constitute a retraction of what was stated in the ad, but Vatican officials interpreted the statements as such and cleared all but two of the signers. These two, Barbara Ferraro and Patricia Hussey, Sisters of Notre Dame at the time, clearly stated that they did not believe in the Roman Catholic position, and that they objected to what they saw as interference of the Roman Catholic church in the reproductive lives of women. They characterized their meetings with representatives of the Vatican as

". . . extremely manipulative, paternalistic, and seductive."[7] No longer members of the Sisters of Notre Dame, Ferraro and Hussey remain active members of the Catholic church, which they envision as a community of believers and a discipleship of equals. The experiences surrounding the signing of the ad have brought them to clarity in regard to their position on abortion. At the time of the signing of the ad, they were asking simply for open dialogue within the church. They are now frankly pro-choice, though not pro-abortion, stating, "We clearly support women's right to choose; women are good moral decision-makers, and clearly, we will stand with women in that choice."[8]

Another woman who has challenged the authority of church men to control women's power over life processes is Mary Ann Sorrentino, former Executive Director of Planned Parenthood of Rhode Island. Her indirect connection with issues of birth control and abortion resulted in her excommunication from the church. In the same session with a parish priest, during which she was informed of this excommunication, her 15-year-old daughter was interrogated about her beliefs regarding abortion. Her right to the sacrament of confirmation rode on her answers. She was confirmed, but subsequently, disillusioned with the treatment her mother received at the hands of church authorities, quit going to church. Mary Ann Sorrentino contested her automatic excommunication, effected, presumably, by what she termed the "self-destruct mechanism called *latae sententiae*."[9] This type of excommunication allows for no inquiry, and is meant to be reserved for the most serious offenses. The simple fact of her position with Planned Parenthood was sufficient to warrant excommunication; no particular action was required on the part of church officials. This is the same device used by Bishop Fabian Bruskewitz in relation to members of Call to Action in the diocese of Lincoln, Nebraska. In regard to Sorrentino's case, an opinion rendered by Father James Coriden, a respected canonist, stated that an automatic excommunication did not apply. This opinion did not impress the bishop of Sorrentino's diocese. She was not to receive communion at the confirmation ceremony of her daughter or at any celebration of the Catholic eucharist.

In her interview with Annie Lally Milhaven, Sorrentino emerges as an independent thinker, who has no intention of leaving the church that has imposed its most serious sanction upon her. "I want to be in this church," she says. "There is something exciting about it, and especially now with all this questioning going on . . . this fuss is not about abortion, it is about women fighting back."[10] She also reveals herself as a woman who has suffered immensely in her determination to be faithful without giving up convictions arrived at after long and serious reflection. Years of pain, she asserts, preceded her decision to speak out. Not without humor, and not without hope, she continues to believe that women's freedom depends on women's control of their own fertility.

The grassroots organization, "Catholics for a Free Choice," shares this conviction. Established in 1973, and led by Fran Kissling since 1982, CFFC ". . . shapes and advances sexual and reproductive ethics that are based on justice, a commitment to women's well-being, and respect for the moral capacity of women and men to make sound and responsible decisions about their lives."[11]

Sorrentino, Hussey and Ferraro, and Gebara mentioned earlier in Chapter 2, join the ranks of numerous men and women from around the world who have suffered at the hands of Vatican and diocesan officials, whose leadership style is too often marked by recourse to warnings, silencing, suppression, firings, inquisitorial investigations and even excommunication. One of the latest to come under suspicion is Richard McBrien of Notre Dame University. The U.S.

Bishops' Secretariat for Doctrine and Pastoral Practices has complained of ambiguities in McBrien's book *Catholicism*, and wants to prevent its use at the undergraduate level and in other religious education programs. The book won the first-place award from the Catholic Press Association in 1995, and has been welcomed as a theological textbook by educators at both the undergraduate and graduate levels. McBrien, like so many others before him, decries the lack of due process, which would give him an opportunity to defend his positions. Too often church leaders seem bent not on healing alienation, but on alienating even further those whose scholarship, ministry, creativity and human experience lead them to fresh interpretations of theology and scripture. The writings of these prophetic individuals touch on a host of sensitive issues, such as power relations, gender issues, infallibility, ordination, sexuality and reproduction. Their insights are rooted in the firm soil of the faith, but these writers look beyond simple formulas in their search for answers to the theological and moral questions that plague us as we enter the 21st century. Together with activists who work for peace and justice, these intellectuals give hope to those who yearn for a church that enlarges and liberates, a church that is no longer inclined to require servility and silence from its members.

So-called progressive Catholics do not resent strong leadership; indeed, they welcome it. Nor do they deny the hierarchy's legitimate concern for sound teaching and unity. They are, however, in search of new models of leadership that reflect values of community, openness, respect for differences, and concern for the continuity of relationships.

New Models of Authority and Leadership

Catholics, and Christians in general, are not alone in their search for leadership styles that nourish and empower. The corporate world is intent on moving away from the authoritarian models that were standard in an industrial age ruled by self-made men perched at the top of clearly delineated chains of command. A general recognition that bureaucracies modeled on military and sports cultures are obsolete has given rise to a host of books and articles insisting on the need for corporations to reinvent themselves if they expect to answer the needs of the new information society.

As it turns out, many of the values considered indispensable for the transformation of business organizations are ones that underlie women's experience and feminist thought. Effective leaders in the age of information, we are told, are those who can operate well in circles of inclusion. They share rather than hoard information and power, opening up channels of access in ways that encourage communication and emphasize collaboration. In reinvented corporations, managers do not insist on status symbols that have traditionally marked off the company's hierarchical divisions. Space arrangements, for example, emphasize flexibility, accessibility and easy communication, instead of providing aloof privacy and distance for corporation leaders. And in this new milieu, success lies not so much in knocking out the competition as in negotiations that profit the interests of all of the negotiating parties.

The emphasis on interrelationships, process and collaboration make of the workplace a more hospitable environment for women accustomed to nurturing these values in the private sphere. When they attain leadership positions, women in charge are much more likely to see themselves at the center of an organizational web rather than at the top of a pyramid of power. They tend to see coworkers as partners in a common enterprise, deserving of trust and respect, rather than as competitors to be kept off-balance and viewed with suspicion. And women, accustomed to adapting quickly to changing circumstances, enjoy an advantage in an economy that calls for innovation and diversity.

In this regard, Mary Catherine Bateson, in her book *Composing a Life,* reflects on the lives of five women who attained high levels of achievement in diverse fields: engineering, psychiatry, jewelry design, research and writing, and university administration. Unlike most men, these women did not follow a narrowly defined career path. Their lives, like those of most women, were marked by conflicting demands and frequent interruptions. As the meaning of work, home, love and commitment changed, these women were obliged to forge a sense of self and a design for their lives out of the improvised materials at hand. They did not have the luxury of single-mindedly pursuing a previously defined vision. Bateson suggests that both men and women can glean valuable lessons from her subjects' ability to deal with ambiguity and multiplicity, to balance tasks and loyalties, to weave together the strands of their personal and professional lives and, in the process, to attain a dearly bought synthesis and harmony, even a certain wisdom. What traditionally were thought to be obstacles in the way of achievement appear now, in the face of the discontinuity, complexity and rapid change that are part of contemporary life, as sources of strength. Bateson muses:

> We can see now that those women who succeed in adopting traditional male models leave the world very much as it is, and so we celebrate the success of women who participate on male terms with a certain ambivalence. We no longer see femaleness as guaranteeing a higher degree of caring; rather, we are concerned with the question of how the necessary combinations of caring will be made and how the old divisions of labor, constructed in terms of spheres of activity, will be redistributed across the genders.[12]

The most progressive organizations in the United States recognize the need and the advantages of introducing women into leadership positions, but the diversification of management (which includes the introduction of racial and various ethnic groups) moves slowly and with difficulty. Prejudice is a stubborn barrier.

One might hope that in the church progress would be swifter, barriers less imposing. Here, after all, there is ideally neither male nor female, neither Greek nor Jew, neither slave nor free. Furthermore, we have historical models that justify women's leadership and their speaking with authority. Consider women's ministry in the New Testament. Or consider the little-known (and, one suspects, deliberately hidden) tradition of abbesses with powers of confession and with quasi-episcopal jurisdiction, a tradition brought to light by Joan Morris in her book *The Lady Was a Bishop*. And today many texts are being uncovered that reveal women who defended their own experience of the divine, and who found in that experience a source of personal authority that circumvented the ecclesial authorities.

The work of Mother Juana de la Cruz is a case in point. This early 16th-century Spanish mystic is not to be confused with the 17th-century Sor Juana Inés de la Cruz, who lived and wrote in Mexico and was discussed in an earlier chapter. Ronald E. Sturtz studies the revelations of the Spanish mystic from the point of view of gender, power and authority. He finds in her a woman who did not hesitate to envision herself as a kind of co-redeemer, empowered to write and preach as men did because, in her view, God was supremely indifferent to sexual roles. Mother Juana places herself and her companions in a long line of women, reaching back to Mary, the mother of Jesus, Mary Magdalen and Elizabeth, who witnessed Christ's miracles. Sturtz comments, "In addition to fulfilling the typically feminine role of visionary, by divine permission and mandate the nun is also called up to play the traditionally masculine role of evangelist."[13]

Catherine of Siena, too, played a traditionally masculine role when she dared to enter the embroiled civil and religious politics of 14th-century Italy. Her passion and force, whether as a mystic, theologian, or convincing advocate for the return of the papacy from Avignon to Rome, were too remarkable to be ignored. And Teresa of Avila, author of the classic *Interior Castle*, loving but determined reformer of her Carmelite order and, together with Catherine of Siena, one of the Doctors of the Church, is a woman who has left her strong imprint on the history of spirituality and of the church.

We could multiply examples of women exercising power and leadership within the church, and it is heartening to remember and celebrate their courage and their service. But their existence does not alter the fact that the church underwent an evolution that centralized power in the hands of a male clergy who exercised it in ways reminiscent of the imperial leaders of the Roman Empire. Once beyond the apostolic age, the church became a stratified household in which wives, women and slaves were to be obedient and submissive. Gender qualifications became more important than spiritual giftedness in determining ministry and leadership. Attempts such as those of Mother Juana de la Cruz to create her own authority ultimately failed. Indeed, the Spanish Inquisition, the 16th-century political instrument set up by the Spanish monarchy to deal with questions of faith, morals and heresy, discredited the religious experiences of female visionaries in general, suggesting that they suffered from delusion. The same body was extremely suspicious of any hint of women appropriating priestly functions.[14] The Spirit blows where she will, however, and today she is inspiring women to claim for themselves rightful authority over their own moral and spiritual lives, and a place in church circles where they can freely and responsibly do theology, interpret scripture, shape liturgy, make policies, nurture parish life, and exercise a wide range of ministries. At the same time women are joining in the discourse on the exercise of power and authority in the church and in the search for models who are faithful to the Gospel and to the realities of today's church and world.

Women and Leadership in Today's Church

Although a wide gap exists between the possibilities for leadership open to women in secular society and within the churches, women in the past 20 years have become a much more visible and vocal presence in many areas of church life. And just as in business, exposure to women's leadership in the church results in increased acceptance and even preference for them. There is, of course, a wide discrepancy among the churches in regard to the level of leadership that women may exercise and, therefore, to the amount of exposure they get. The Catholic church bars women from ordination, thereby excluding them from the influence and decision-making powers that attach to holy orders. Most mainstream Protestant churches have opened the ranks of the ordained to women, giving them the right to preach and teach, and to share in the sacramental power that is granted with ordination, thus assuring them inclusion in the governing structure of their churches. In some denominations, a few women have been ordained bishops. There is no church, however, in which full equality has been attained and assured. Discrimination, sometimes strong and blatant, sometimes subtle but no less effective, survives in many forms.   In some of the mainstream Protestant churches, for instance, newly ordained men find their way quickly, for the most part, into parishes where they are often received as pastors, while women seeking ministerial positions may have to wait two years or more to be placed. When they are placed, they are less likely to be pastors, and they often find themselves in smaller parishes in rural areas. Some women, seeking ministerial positions, are diverted to child-care centers, social agencies and counseling. It is still not uncommon for men to receive higher salaries than women in the same positions, and allowances granted to men for travel, conferences and the like can be double the allowance for women pastors.

In the Episcopal church, the ordination of women to the priesthood and to the episcopate still meets with deep resistance. Traditionalist enclaves reacted with inflammatory fervor at the prospect of Barbara Harris' consecration as a bishop in 1988 in the diocese of Massachusetts. When she was in fact installed as bishop, six diocesan bishops and three retired bishops declared they would be unable to consider themselves in communion with her as a bishop or to accept episcopal actions performed by her. Pamela W. Darling describes their course as ". . . somewhere between rebellion and schism."[15] The protesting bishops chose not to break away from the Episcopal church, but they made a concerted effort to call the church back to the "true faith," which apparently excludes women's leadership, if it does not require complete subordination. Failing in their attempt to depict the ordination of a woman as bishop as invalid, traditionalists continue to use other ploys to protect themselves from the jurisdiction of women bishops or those ordained by them. The *Washington Post* of January 15, 1996, for instance, recounts the experience of Bishop Jane Holmes Dixon, who was sent by Washington's Bishop Ronald H. Haines to celebrate Mass at the conservative St. Luke's Episcopal Church in Bladensburg, Md. No one had prepared the altar with the necessary communion wafers, wine or candles, and there were no worshippers from the parish in the pews at first, except three hostile observers who clearly did not expect to participate in the service. The pastor of St. Luke's had written to Haines to protest the visit, calling it ". . . a violation of our consciences." He stopped short of locking the doors of the church, because Dixon had pledged to hold the service outside the church on Route 450 if he did so. Dixon was supported by about 45 Episcopalians who came from other sections of the Washington area, and by about seven church members of St. Luke's, who joined the worshippers as the service began. Examples such as this remind us that even when women attain episcopal status, the struggle for real equality and for warm acceptance continues.

The Catholic church, at least in its hierarchical representatives, is still in the position of gratefully accepting women's service, praising their genius, and denying them real power. There are no women in the governing structure of the Holy See, and none among the College of Cardinals which elects the Pope. No woman, whatever her pastoral and spiritual gifts or theological education, may preside at the Eucharist. Indeed, the bishops of at least two U.S. dioceses, and some pastors, still balk at the idea of altar girls, even though the Vatican has lifted the ban against them. Bishop Bruskewitz of Lincoln, Nebraska is quoted as saying:

> I thought I'd wait and see if those dioceses which have altar girls have seminaries that are packed with candidates and convents that are filled with novices and 100 percent of the Catholics at Mass, and so on. If all of that comes about because of altar girls, I would certainly look at our situation in a new light.[16]

This seems a heavy burden to lay on the slim shoulders of the girls of his diocese, one he spares boys who wish to serve.

The exclusion of women from the most influential levels of leadership in the church coexists with statements affirming the equality of women and men. As a statement released by the Women-Church Convergence notes, however, no document issued from the Vatican makes a simple and unambiguous declaration in regard to the equality of the sexes.[17] In the report made to the U.N. on the eve of the Fourth World Conference on Women held in Beijing, for instance, John Paul II reiterated his position that while women and men enjoy "equal dignity in all areas of life," they do not have "an equality of roles and functions."[18] The Women-Church Convergence rightly traces this questionable distinction to an outdated patriarchal anthropology, which roots men's dignity in the simple fact of their humanity and women's in their reproductive and mothering capacity. Men remain the norm in this outlook; women are derivative and "different."[19]

In an attempt to bridge the gap between the language of equality and the practice of excluding women from ordination, and recognizing the growing impatience and disillusionment not only of women but of all who want a full and honest response to the gospel call to equality, Pope John Paul II in a recent document spoke of the urgent necessity ". . . to take certain concrete steps, beginning by providing room for women to participate in different fields and at all levels, including decision-making processes, above all in matters which concern women themselves." [20]

This statement appears in the papal response to the Synod on Consecrated Life, which took place in Rome in October 1994. At that meeting, the African Bishop Ernest Kombo stated that women should have access to the highest posts of the church hierarchy and should be named cardinals. To date, John Paul II has not taken the concrete step of introducing women into this particular level of decision-making. To do so would be to profoundly disturb power relations within the church. Women, we hope, would not simply take their place in an unchanged bureaucratic maze, but would continue to challenge church polity, liturgical rites, the theological and ethical frameworks of our faith, the language we use to speak of God, and ideas about sexuality, authority and right relationship in community. They would, we hope, continue to disrupt dominance rather than assume it. Still, is it realistic to imagine that women cardinals, if they should appear in some faraway, future scenario, will be the spiritual heirs of Rosemary Radford Ruether, Elisabeth Schüssler Fiorenza, or Sandra Schneiders? Isn't it more likely that challenges, such as those mentioned above, will continue to come, not from the centers of power, but from the margins?

In any case, women are not waiting for an invitation to be ordained or appointed as cardinals in order to exercise leadership within the church. Historically, women religious led the way in establishing a system of Catholic schools and Catholic hospitals, which still serve the needs of Americans of every faith and social class. Today women, lay and religious alike, are helping to reshape Catholic life, if not at the centers of power, then at the periphery. Women theologians are beginning to free theology from androcentric bonds and the church from patriarchal constraints. Women in large numbers have entered the field of spiritual direction, opening the way for women (and men as well) to discover new paths to God, new ways of integrating body, mind and soul, a new vocabulary of the Spirit, and a new confidence in attaining self-definition. They offer a wide range of prayer experiences and spiritual reflection as directors of retreat centers. Parish life is feeling the effect of women in the roles of director of religious education, liturgical ministers, parish administrators, and leaders of study and prayer groups. Women, indeed, constitute 85% of parish ministers. Dioceses are welcoming more women as editors of diocesan papers, members of marriage tribunals and women's commissions, chancellors, heads of diocesan offices and vicars of religious. They serve in senior staff positions for the National Conference of Catholic Bishops, and head three of the secretariats of that body. Women are playing an important role in the area of social justice advocacy, whether through their religious congregations or through organizations such as the 8th Day Center, based in Chicago, and

Network, a Washington-based lobbying group. And they play a leadership role in providing shelter for abused and homeless women, literacy skills and other social services for the economically disadvantaged, and ministry to people living with AIDS.

The women who comprise the Women-Church Convergence exercise another kind of leadership role within and on the edges of the church. The Convergence describes itself as "a national (United States) coalition of women's groups and organizations rooted in the Roman Catholic tradition and committed to furthering the goals of the Women-Church movement. It is feminist in commitment and global in outreach." Women-Church stands in opposition to hierarchical forms of domination, seeking to model a "discipleship of equals," the phrase coined by Elisabeth Schüssler Fiorenza to characterize the early Christian communities. It provides a space where women, claiming their own autonomy, can speak freely out of their own experience, rather than within male-defined categories which deny women speech and power. In the welcoming environment of Women-Church, feminist discourse waxes strong, feminist theology and hermeneutics flourish, and feminist liturgies find free expression. The women who identify with Women-Church intend neither to leave the church nor to continue to accept a subordinate place within it. They seek to free the church from the dehumanizing effects of patriarchy and to make of it a true household of freedom and reconciliation. Rosemary Radford Ruether writes in connection with the concept of Women-Church:

> Women are not authentically included in Church unless Church means a community that seeks to overcome patriarchy as the root expression of oppressive relations between men and women, between generations, and between those who are powerful and those who are weak. Patriarchy means the elabo-

ration of these natural distinctions into sources of privilege and dehumanization. The very concept of the Church as an exodus community from sin and evil, living in hope of redeemed humanity on a redeemed earth, implies the overcoming of patriarchy and its false sacralization as the *ecclesia* of patriarchy.[21]

The struggle on the part of women to overcome patriarchy has involved the forging of a new language and new concepts, which are slowly freeing women from the assumptions of a male-dominated culture. The effort has brought them into the public realm, where their presence as leaders, still extremely limited, gives them some liberty to experiment with new ways of using authority and power. Still trying to reconcile being woman with entertaining thoughts of creation, achievement and ambition, and still repelled by the kind of abusive power of which they have been too often the victims, women are joining in the search for new models of leadership.

Leadership for the New Millennium

The future cries out for models of leadership that accentuate mutuality, creativity and commitment, rather than control. The past is not devoid of such models. A striking one can be found in the pages of scripture. Jesus, in his person and in his teaching, dramatically reversed classical notions of authority and power. He was firm in his rejection of power as exercised in the patriarchal tradition, a rejection his own followers found difficult to understand. He told the disciples, who were arguing about who should be regarded as greatest, "Earthly kings lord it over their people . . . it cannot be that way with you. . . . I am in your midst as the one who serves you" (Lk 22:24-28).

The servant Jesus could also say with full assurance that authority had been given to him both in heaven and on earth (Mk 28:18). It was clear, however, that he had no intention of wielding it in the manner of monarchs. He invited rather than coerced people into the new dispensation. He was capable of clear-eyed judgment and of anger – not hesitating to call hypocrites "whited sepulchers," for instance – but his ordinary stance toward sinners and toward outcasts was one of compassion, healing and forgiveness. He did not scorn the legal system of the Jewish tradition, but dispensed with legal regulations when they stood in the way of human need. In this spirit, his disciples were instructed not to lay impossible burdens on the backs of believers. Those who listened to his words recognized his authority at the same time that they experienced his loving compassion, his patience, his forgiveness, and his solidarity with the least among them.

The renegade monk in Shusaku Endo's *The Samurai* recognizes Jesus' solidarity with the poor in the person of the Indians among whom he has made his home. He tries to make the Japanese envoys to Mexico understand his loyalty and love for the ugly, emaciated Jesus whom they scorn. "Had he lived an exalted, powerful life beyond our grasp, I would not feel like this about him," he explains, and continues:

> He understands the hearts of the wretched, because
> His entire life was wretched. He knows the agonies
> of those who die a terrible death, because He died in
> misery. He was not in the least powerful. He was not
> beautiful.[22]

Women approach this image of Jesus as the weak, powerless and suffering servant with understandable caution. History and cultural conditioning have cast them too readily in the role of self-sacrificing victims, destined to abort their own growth to full personhood in the interest of helping the men in their lives attain theirs. They nevertheless have a profound understanding and appreciation of the concepts of leadership as service, and power as the establishment of right relationships governed ultimately by love.

The lessons of Jesus were not lost on his early disciples. Authority and leadership among them were not vested in a sacred few by reason of their office, but were open to all in whose lives the mystery of Christ and the gifts of the Spirit were clearly manifest. These gifts were not limited in terms of gender, class or race; neither did these factors limit access to authority, leadership and power. Just as with ministry, however, authority and leadership gradually came to be associated with office. Eventually the Pope, like the pretenders to "divine" monarchy, claimed absolute power, a power nevertheless shared with bishops whose legislative, judicial and executive authority within their own dioceses was and is virtually complete. For centuries, lay people were effectively removed from decision-making at the diocesan level, and even at the parish level, where a domineering pastor could exercise autocratic control, not only over his parishioners, but over his priest associates as well.

Vatican II called for decentralization, dialogue and consultation, and there has been significant movement in this direction. But habits of thought and practice developed over centuries die hard, and the church is still capable of defending historical forms of authority that have lost relevance. In some dioceses, two visions of church and authority seem to be on a collision course. The visions are described by Leonardo Boff as the church looking outward and the church looking inward. The first represents:

> . . . what is highest and most holy in the mystery of humanity and God. It embodies humanity's hope that not everything has come under the domination of self-interested power structures. The Church inspires confidence and the Gospel joy of life and hope.

The second stance:

> . . . is focused on intrasystemic relationships; Christians
> are steeped in venerable traditions, liturgical prescrip-
> tions, well-defined moral codes, ecclesiastical struc-
> tures, and forms of power – all powerfully controlled
> and centralized by a body of experts, the hierarchy.
> Tensions, conflicts, and instances of authoritarianism
> arise on this internal level. . . . [23]

As we approach the third millennium, there is broader
and more vigorous resistance to powerful control exercised
from the center in ways that disregard basic respect for
human rights, healthy differences of opinion, and the capacity of the church as people of God to share in the priestly
and prophetic mission of Jesus. There is a corresponding
call for a return to a Gospel understanding of authority and
power as intimately related to service and love. "Domineering over your faith is not my purpose," Paul wrote to the
Corinthians. "I prefer to work with you toward your happi-
ness" (2 Cor. 1:24).

The association of power and authority with service
and love leads many to assert that women are particularly
well-suited to be leaders in church and society in the coming
millennium, but there is some debate about whether gender
really affects the way one conceives of and exercises power.
Some argue that biocultural influences condition men to
favor impersonal hierarchies, rigid theology, legalistic ethics,
competitiveness, and jealous guarding over decision-making.
Women's conditioning, on the other hand, leads them to
prefer personal and open communities, flexible theology,
situational or existential ethics, and responsible, democratic
decision-making. Others argue that women and men are
much more alike than different in positions of power, as in
everything else, and that gender seems not to be a reliable

predictor of whether a person will behave in ways labelled "masculine" or "feminine."

Perhaps in time there will be sufficient empirical documentation to determine whether there are significant sex-based differences in the way women and men approach leadership. In any case, it is well to keep in mind that a whole complex of factors help shape one's approach to authority and leadership: gender, race, class, education, values, and sense of self are among them. Meanwhile, rather than strive to emphasize or deemphasize a male/female dichotomy, it would seem more productive to acknowledge the wide range of leadership styles that exists among both women and men. Both should be exquisitely attuned to the shift in the structure of gender power relations that is currently under way; both should be called to act in ways that accord with gospel values.

The gospel's overriding values, as we saw in the example of Jesus, are those of freedom and service without domination. The early Christians witness to the possibility of free, egalitarian, inclusive communities, where the needs of any one become the concern of all. While there may have been strife and struggle as the early Christian communities strove to live out their ideals, there was no hint among their leaders of a punitive mentality, manipulation, secrecy or repression. There is nothing to legitimate the kind of control, whether imposed by women or men, that stifles creative thought or builds walls around dogmas and practices that made sense in a certain culture at a certain time, but which no longer serve the interests of the church.

Christian feminists, in their reading both of scripture and of the moment of history which is ours, call for a rethinking of what constitutes power, authority, and leadership. If the Christian community, indeed the entire human community, is to thrive, power must be understood not as something to be hoarded, but as something to be shared.

Authority must be understood not only as the prerogative of elected and appointed leaders, but also as a personal attribute which has its source in our own experience. And leaders must be situated, not at the "top," but at the center of things, eliciting and giving wide scope to the gifts of all.

In feminist theory, chains of command give way to circles. The familiar ranking – God first, then angels, men, women (with place assigned for both sexes by race, ethnicity, and class), animals, plants and rocks – breaks down into a network of interdependence. Exploitative and manipulative forms of power surrender to nurturant forms that foster growth and autonomy.[24] In this view, according to Letty M. Russell:

> Authority is exercised *in* community and not *over* community and tends to reinforce ideas of coopera- tion, with contributions from a wide diversity of persons enriching the whole.[25]

This model, of course, stands in vivid contrast to the dominator model. Feminists join many in church and society who believe that we have reached the logical limits of a model characterized by hierarchic, authoritarian and violent modes of interaction. Indeed, feminism is a key counterforce to the mentality of domination – a mentality that has brought us to the point where all life on our globe is threatened. Overcoming it involves a revolution in the way we think of women and men and the way we organize relations between them. Overcoming it will involve a great deal more, but this is basic. We cannot continue to equate "real" men with strength, often expressed through brutality and violence, and believe that this can be tolerated because women balance the scales by their life-generating and life-sustaining qualities. Instead, women and men alike will have to begin to equate power – a power rightly claimed by women and men of every race and exercised by them in the private and public realms alike – with responsibility, love and nurturance.

One should expect to find in the church models of this kind of leadership and the power and authority that attend it. And the church does provide striking examples of the kind of leadership that fosters trust, growth and diversity. Women religious have spent the last 30 years creating structures that reflect their desire for participative forms of government and models of shared leadership. The base communities of Central and Latin America offer impressive examples of power as service and of leadership fostered and exercised at the local level. Many parishes are intentional in adopting a team model of leadership and in tapping into the manifold gifts of parishioners. The latter are included in decision-making processes that determine the use of resources, the services needed in the parish, the kind of liturgy that best suits the congregation, and the type of outreach that expresses their desire to be in solidarity with the oppressed. And some bishops, notwithstanding a shift to the right in many aspects of church life among Roman Catholics, remain faithful to the principles enunciated at Vatican Council II. They consult with the people of their diocese, encourage rather than repress movements of reform, welcome lay leadership, and publicly support women's full participation in the life of the church. These bishops are, unfortunately, few in number.

Despite these examples and the vigorous rethinking within the church as to the nature and use of power and authority, business sometimes appears to be taking the lead in introducing new models of leadership. For profit-making reasons of their own, many corporations are encouraging methods that stress interrelating teams rather than high profile, egotistical leaders surrounded by symbols of status. They are beginning to see the wisdom of women's efforts to bridge the gap that some suppose to exist between work

and community, the private and the professional, the effi-
cient and the humane. A kind of managerial revolution is
replacing lone-hero type executives with people who place
a high premium on collaboration, the free flow of information, careful listening to the work force, and a concern for
means as well as ends.

Margaret J. Wheatley addresses corporate manager
types in her book *Leadership and the New Science*, but her
observations are equally relevant to church leadership in an
age of disequilibrium, conflict, and change. Wheatley looks
to quantum physics, self-organizing systems, and chaos
theory for hints about how the universe manages the interplay of order and change, autonomy and control. She notes
the uses of disorder in creating new possibilities for growth,
and gleans lessons from fractals, the beautifully intricate
shapes that nature creates ". . . by enumerating a few basic
principles and then permitting great amounts of autonomy."[26]

Wheatley convinces us that organizations and their
leaders, especially in an age of transition, would do well to
study and imitate nature's ability to adapt structures to
changing environments, to let power balances shift, and to
surrender control for trust in dynamic interconnectedness.
It is interesting to find in this work, hailed as the best
management book of the year, frequent references to the
centrality of relationship in all of life and to the relevance
for organizational life of the human longing for community,
meaning, dignity and love. Wheatley does not hesitate to
assert that power gets its charge, whether positive or negative, from the quality of relationships, and that "Love in
organizations . . . is the most potent source of power we
have available."[27]

Whether in business or in the church, leadership in the
new millennium will focus less on concern with hierarchies,
permanence and unruffled organization and more on chan-

nels for the exchange of power and energy. Effective leaders will appreciate diversity and thrive on meaning derived from multiple sources. They will welcome wide participation in organizational matters, recognizing involvement as a source of energy. They will be open to inquiry and slow to restrain change or repress innovation. Organizations that endure will have fluid, resilient forms and permeable boundaries.

These messages are coming from numerous sources today: among them, theology, scripture, sociology, management theory and the new science. The lessons are reinforced by our contemporary experience, but they are not entirely new. The church that has survived as an organization for two millennia has enjoyed considerable success in the art of maintaining identity while changing form. It has proven itself capable of self-renewal at crucial points throughout its history. At this particular point, as we stand poised at the threshold of the year 2000, the church will be most alive in those places where it is most open to new information and new forms, most patient with ambiguity, most eager to enter into fruitful partnerships, most inimical to paradigms of patriarchy, most welcoming of diversity, most inclusive of women, most empowering; in a word, most free and loving.

Endnotes

1. *Good Bones and Simple Murders* (New York: Doubleday, 1994), 27-28.
2. Dorothy Dinnerstein, *The Mermaid and the Minotaur* (New York: Harper and Row, 1976), 225.
3. *On Becoming a Leader* (New York: Addison-Wesley Pub. Co., Inc., 1989), 50-51.
4. Carolyn G. Heilbrun, *Writing a Woman's Life* (New York: Ballantine Books, 1988), 55.
5. *Ibid.*, 44.

6. "A New Spelling of our Name," in *Front Line Feminism, 1975-1995: Essays from Sojourner's First 20 Years*, ed. Karen Kahn (San Francisco: Aunt Lute Books, 1995), 30.

7. Annie Lally Milhaven, ed., The Inside Stories: 13 Valiant Women Challenging the Church (Mystic, Conn.: Twenty-Third Publications, 1987), 229.

8. *Ibid.,* 234.

9. *Ibid.,* 250.

10. *Ibid.,* 253-254.

11. For further information about this organization contact Catholics for a Free Choice, 1436 U Street NW, Suite 301, Washington, D.C. 20009.

12. Mary Catherine Bateson, *Composing a Life* (New York: Penguin Books, 1990), 233.

13. *The Guitar of God: Gender, Power, and Authority in the Visionary World of Mother Juana de la Cruz (1481-1534)* (Philadelphia: University of Pennsylvania Press, 1990), 123.

14. *Ibid.,* note 31, 12.

15. *New Wine: The Story of Women Transforming Leadership and Power in the Episcopal Church* (Boston: Cowling Publications, 1994), 175.

16. *National Catholic Reporter,* 12 April 1996, 7.

17. "Equal is as Equal Does" (*Women-Church Convergence*, 1995), 2.

18. The Vatican Report to the U.N., paragraph 2a; quoted in "Equal Is as Equal Does," 2.

19. "Equal Is as Equal Does," 2-3.

20. Vita Consecrata, ch. II, 7.

21. *Women-Church: Theology and Practice of Feminist Liturgical Com-munities* (San Francisco: Harper and Row, 1985), 64.

22. *The Samurai,* trans. Van C. Gessel (New York: Vintage Books, 1984), 220.

23. *Church: Charism and Power,* trans. John W. Diercksmeier (New York: Crossroad, 1985), 47.

24. See Joan Chittister's *Job's Daughters: Women and Power* (New York: Paulist Press, 1990), 11-51 for an analysis of Rollo May's types of power as they apply to women.

25. *Household of Freedom: Authority in Feminist Theology* (Philadelphia: The Westminster Press, 1987), 34-35.

26. Margaret J. Wheatley, *Leadership and the New Science: Learning about Organization from an Orderly Universe* (San Francisco: Berrett-Koehler Publications, 1994), xii.

27. *Ibid.,* 39.

Conclusion

I set out in this book to explore the extent to which we may speak of the feminization of the church. Recognizing that the term is an ambiguous one, I examined some of the meanings attached to it, and spelled out what I mean by a feminized church. The church's feminization, as I understand it, will be complete when women's presence, voice, experience, history, gifts, energy and creativity are fully recognized and given free rein, and when women's power in the church is commensurate with their service and responsibility.

I have argued that a transformed consciousness among women in the church is even now bringing about its feminization. The tool that is shaping the process is what Mary Fainsod Katzenstein has termed "discursive politics." She describes it as:

> . . . the politics of meaning-making. It is discursive in that it seeks to reinterpret, reformulate, rethink, and rewrite the norms and practices of society and the state. . . . Its premise is that conceptual changes directly bear on material ones. Discursive politics relies heavily but not exclusively on language. Its vehicle is both speech and print – conversations, debate, conferences, essays, stories, newsletters, books.[1]

These, indeed, are the means that women in the church, and particularly feminists, are using. They are forging new meanings and constructing a new language to express their evolving understanding of themselves and of their relation to the church. And while these exchanges appear not to have had notable effect on the upper reaches of the hierarchy, Katzenstein outlines three areas in which feminist discursive politics has had a transforming effect: "(1) the empowerment of women religious; (2) the change in popular attitudes toward gender issues in the church; (3) the influence over the agenda of church authorities."[2] Some, indeed, feel feminists enjoy an *unwarranted* power to determine the church's agenda. One of the Vatican's apostolic delegates is reported to have said, only partly in jest, according to Katzenstein, that the Pope doesn't seem to realize that feminism makes Washington a hardship post. And James Hitchcock, a conservative Catholic commentator, claims that despite John Paul II's appointment of reactionary bishops, liberal priests and "unwavering feminists" still call the shots in too many parishes and church offices.[3] While women's power to make decisions in the church may be limited, their power to set the agenda of public debate in the church, and their power to transform the myth, language and symbols that shape the way people think, pray and define their concerns is considerable, and is a force in bringing about the church's feminization.

This feminization implies neither a turn to a sentimental faith removed from the world's struggles, nor a take-over by women of essentially unchanged patriarchal structures. It implies, rather, the realization of a feminist vision of real equality, inclusion and mutuality. The church feminized will be a renewed church where freedom, reciprocity and shared power replace oppressive control. In this sense, the feminization of culture and of the church will be synonymous with their humanization. When it is accomplished, the term "feminization" will lose its meaning. We will have overcome all of the dualisms that it implies.

Meanwhile, the transformation of women's consciousness will proceed apace. We will continue to examine the ways we relate to God, ourselves, men, children, work and home, church and society. Striving to become whole, we will join with all who envision the possibility of a world beyond divisions, beyond patriarchy. Our freeing of ourselves will contribute to human liberation, and to furthering a delicate sensitivity to the web that connects the human species and all of creation.

Pie in the sky? Not to those who believe in the power of the Spirit; not to those committed to resolute resistance and compassionate solidarity; not to those convinced of the vigor and strength of prophetic imagination.

Endnotes

1. See her excellent analysis of discursive politics at work in the Catholic church in "Discursive Politics and Feminist Activism in the Catholic Church," in *Feminist Organizations: Harvest of the New Women's Movement*, eds. Myra Marx Ferree and Patricia Yancey Martin (Philadelphia: Temple University Press, 1995), 35-52.
2. *Ibid.*, 45.
3. *San Francisco Chronicle*, 20 June 1996, "John Paul Puts Mark on Church."

Appendix

Publisher's Note

In this special appendix, the reader will find five responses to the ideas advanced by Kaye Ashe in *The Feminization of the Church?* The objective is to give the reader other vantage points from which to view the presentation, a chance to stop and reflect on a set of issues whose importance is matched only by its complexity. The hoped-for effect is to give the book additional context, the sense that the thesis is coming from not just a single author but from the reflection and discussion going on in a larger community. The five respondents are respected and experienced voices of women and men from within the pastoral, intellectual and leadership dimensions of today's Church. Their comments may serve to anticipate further stages in the unfolding and always unfinished dialectic taking place over the role of women in the Catholic Church.

This book is a resource for all those whose prayer, study and experience are telling them that world culture is changing dramatically and that, through the process of feminization described and celebrated here, the Spirit is characteristically moving out ahead of the Church to reveal what is most authentic in human experience. Kaye Ashe invites you to join the voices she has invited to share in this ongoing colloquy about how to help move our Church into the future. Visit our website at http://www.natcath.com and leave your e-mail comments at sheedward@aol.com or direct your correspondence to Sheed & Ward, 115 E. Armour Blvd., Kansas City, MO., 64111.

Chapter 1: Women and Spirituality

As Kaye indicates, all experience is gendered. However, beyond that generic statement, it is difficult to be precise without perpetuating stereotypes. The assumption becomes that we can differentiate between men and women on a basis other than the biological alone. But this is no easy task. We can be descriptive, that most men, etc., and most women, etc., but even that way of speaking indicates a lack of assurance on our part about what the differences between the genders might be. For are those differences intrinsic? To what degree do they truly differentiate? Why describe them in terms of gender at all? Are they not *human* differences? We must affirm men and women as *equal* partners in the human project, but are we not simply attempting in the end to discover what it means to be *human*?

For example, as we attempt to contrast the spiritualities of the desert, of Thomas à Kempis, of Ignatius with more feminized spiritualities, are these spiritualities as much a question of their epoch or period of history as of their gender? Have their spiritualities been shaped more by their period of history and their individuality than by gender? What makes them "male" other than the fact that they are men? At least the factors of historicality and individuality are of comparable significance.

Sor Juana insisted that the soul and mind were *without* gender. In the song in honor of St. Catherine of Alexandria, she gives witness "that gender is not of the essence in matter of intelligence." How important then is gender? It *is* important because half of the human race has been denied their right to full and equal participation in the human journey. But if that changes, would gender be a factor? We must oppose the exclusion of women as equal partners in social and ecclesial life, but this does not mean that there is a women's spirituality, only that spirituality needs to be feminized, to follow Kaye's understanding of that term as the full inclusion of women. The full inclusion of women is one thing, paramount, not to be compromised, but the identification of the particular distinctiveness of 'women' and 'men' another. Certainly any movement with hope or promise for the future must be inclusive and grounded in the equality of both sexes. But what we precisely mean by gender still remains an open question.

Is the search for feminist spiritualities then really a search for more whole spiritualities – spiritualities that may have an equal appeal to men as well? And are not some contemporary efforts at developing feminist spirituality potentially unwhole or unbalanced as some of the classical spiritualities we have inherited? Woman's spirituality and woman's power, yes. But does that mean to say that the spirituality is gendered or simply more fully human?

Donald J. Goergen, OP
Aquinas Institute of Theology, St. Louis, Mo.

Chapter 2: Women and Ethics

Two issues that strike me as important for future reflection concern Ashe's reflections on anger in the service of justice, and the relationship between respect for women and respect for the environment.

We in the Christian tradition often forget that anger, as an emotion that has the creator-God as its ultimate source, is in and of itself good. In particular, anger is that which can provide us with the concrete physical and psychological motivation to act against the injustice that is its object. Jesus, after all, was angry on more than one occasion. Women must learn that anger is acceptable; women must *learn* to be angry at those injustices that impact them and those whom they care about. Anger in the service of justice, of course, must be formed by an enlightened practical reason, as well as by justice and love, and must be directed at its appropriate objects. As Ashe points out, a steady diet of undirected or misdirected anger is self-destructive; it is also counterproductive with regard to its goal of achieving justice.

And this, it seems to me, is a very real problem in today's Church. People often take offense when they are the objects of anger, especially if they do not feel themselves responsible for the wrongs against which the anger is directed. Those supporting crucial concerns of women in the Church and society must be careful to direct their anger to issues and situations, rather (in most cases) than to individuals. The anger that is called for in today's Church – the anger of women in particular – must also be tempered by good humor and the recognized ability to be self-critical. Anger alone is not enough to accomplish change, but it can be a powerful motivator for establishing those kinds of critical, mutual relationships with others that can change perception, and, hence, action.

A short word on Ashe's linking of respect for women with respect for the environment; her insights not only reflect a truth about the character of male hegemony, but also may serve a more practical purpose as well. A number of men who are not particularly sensitive (for a number of reasons) to women's issues are indeed attuned to environmental ones. In this context, it is very important to link the two closely together – respect for the latter may open the door to understanding the larger structural issues that have led to neglect of the former.

Daniel Syverstad, O.P.
Prior provincial of the Province
of the Holy Name of Jesus
Oakland, Calif.

Chapter 3: Women and Language

In her introduction to the book, Kaye Ashe states that her intent is "to examine the potential of feminist analysis to bring the Church and its members to greater wholeness." The arena of language is critical in this examination precisely because language enables one to become conscious and self-reflective. Language names reality and indeed creates it. Without language, we would not have the ability to interpret events. The entire sacramental nature of the Church is built around the word-action dynamic.

Further, each of us experiences the reality of words that heal and words that bruise, words that enliven and words that kill, words that encourage as well as words that discourage. Our experience proves forever false the adage sung by children: "Sticks and stones may break my bones, but names will never hurt me."

Ashe brings a wealth of knowledge gathered from literature, philosophy, scripture and women's studies that show how our language has rendered women invisible and demeaned their experience. Because we have lived in a male-dominated society, most of us, both men and women, tend to be unconscious of this reality. The generic-pronoun, the rule of male precedence, the trivialization of woman-talk, the selectivity of Lectionary readings all portray male experience as human experience. It has become the norm from which all other experience is judged. This is the root meaning of sexism. What has become "normative" for us must become relativized.

One can only welcome the awakening of feminine consciousness as a move toward wholeness within the human community no matter the discomfort that it creates. Ashe herself states that questions in the women's movement touch the nerve-center of the human condition. It is understandable that the nerve becomes raw when we bring these questions into ecclesial life and our language of God. Nothing is more intimate to the human soul than its communion with God. When one begins to tinker with language that names God and gives expression to worship, emotions are bound to skyrocket. The faith-community must be both attentive and cautious.

While Ashe does a great service in demonstrating that cultural bias has done incredible damage, and while much of this can be remedied now, there is still the fact that our Christian faith is a revealed faith. No one's human experience contains it, except that of Jesus. For example, while care must be taken not to see "Abba, Father" as the sole metaphor for God, it is legitimate to ask if this title does not have a privileged position because it best expressed the experience of Jesus.

It is a delicate balance to be open to the new human (feminist) experience and the Church's authentic tradition. It is necessary to discern carefully the distinction between what is truly progress and not a foregone conclusion as theologians from any particular persuasion might intimate. Because such questions do not touch on the nerve-center of faith life, only time coupled with healthy, respectful and strong debate (under the guidance of the Holy Spirit) will gradually lead us to a deeper and truer understanding of God's revelation in Jesus, and therefore to a greater ecclesial wholeness. The Church is undergoing this painful and exciting dialectic. Sister Kaye Ashe has significantly contributed to this debate. Indeed, to use the words of Mary Collins, "we are dealing with radical theological and ecclesial questions," questions that may take a century to resolve.

Edward M. Ruane, O.P.
Prior provincial of the Province of
St. Albert the Great, Chicago, IL

Chapter 4: Women and Ministry

The admission of Gentiles to the Church furnishes an instructive parallel to the feminization of the Church's ministry. Authority has declared the ordination of women to be impossible, even though Jesus said nothing about the matter. Jesus, however, did say, "I was sent only to the lost sheep of the House of Israel" (Matthew 15:24), and ordered his disciples, "Go nowhere among the Gentiles and enter no town of the Samaritans, but go rather to the lost sheep of the House of Israel" (Matthew 10:6).

Jesus, in other words, declared that his divine mission was restricted to Jews, and insisted that his followers should not attempt to convert Gentiles. Yet within twenty years converts of pagan origin were the majority believers, and they did not first have to become Jews (Galatians 2:1-10).

The first step in this process was the recognition by Paul and others that the positive response of Gentiles to the gospel meant that they were graced. They had been chosen by God. The second step was the fact that Jesus had made exceptions to his own rule. He praised the faith of a Gentile woman (Matthew 15:28) and of a pagan centurion (Matthew 8:10, Luke 7:9) and worked miracles for both of them. These episodes were interpreted as Jesus' recognition of the action of the Holy Spirit in non-Jews. These exceptions opened the door to the mission to the Gentiles.

The accession of women to the highest levels of ministry within the Church is a much easier issue, precisely because there is no dominical prohibition. No one can deny the action of the Holy Spirit in the ministries that women have been permitted to exercise. To exclude others is unjustified. If it is claimed that Jesus' intention is evidenced by his exclusive choice of men as his apostles (Mark 3:16-19), it must be conceded that he also provided the same sort of loophole that made the conversion of Gentiles possible. He chose Mary Magdalene as the premier apostle of the resurrection (John 20:11-18). In other words, Jesus showed that women can perform the precise ministry for which the Twelve were chosen.

Jerome Murphy-O'Connor, O.P.
Ecole Biblique, Jerusalem

Chapter 5: Women and Leadership

Kaye Ashe presents well the capacity of women for leadership and some of our successes and struggles with its exercise. She notes the emphasis that the pope and U.S. bishops have recently given to the importance of ecclesial leadership by women. *Creating a Home*, a publication by the Leadership Conference of Women Religious, is a valuable resource on this topic.

Because the words *power, authority* and *leadership* have multiple, overlapping definitions, it would have been helpful had Ashe described more clearly how she understands each term. Theoretical and practical difficulties emerge precisely in the interpretation and application of these concepts. Too often power, authority and leadership are conceived of as finite quantities rather than as relational qualities exercised differently in various arenas. What is the relationship between personal power, authority and leadership talents, and the way these are exercised within the many systems to which every person belongs?

A core dilemma is the relationship between autonomy and mutuality, values which seem to be simply juxtaposed in this chapter. Women must be moral agents and decision-makers, subjects rather than objects. Does autonomy differ, however, from the individualism espoused by liberal philosophy or is it a term from certain feminist theories which are grounded in liberal individualism? Postmodern insights in science and psychology probe the ineluctable relationality of everything that exists. According to this view, power is relational, both receptive and creative. The prized category in such fields as the new cosmology and trinitarian ecclesiology is creative freedom in, through and for relationships. In *From a Broken Web,* Catherine Keller contrasts the autonomous, atomistic self with the creative-relationship self in which there is a continual integration of all the relationships in which the self exists.

The example of Mary Ann Sorrentino illustrates this dilemma. What does it mean to belong freely to a community of moral and religious discourse and practice and also to be director of a group whose practices and discourse are diametrically opposed to this community in critical matters? Are there simple issues of power, procedures, process and sanctions involved or are these also matters of critical and contradictory moral judgments and practices? What are the requirements of right relationships?

Patricia Walter, O.P.
Prioress of the Adrian Dominican Congregation

Works Cited

Introduction

Douglas, Ann. *The Feminization of American Culture.* New York: Doubleday, Anchor Books Edition, 1988.

Glaser, John W. "Epoch III: the church feminized." *Commonweal* (28 January 1983).

Gudorf, Christine E. "Renewal or Repatriarchalization? Responses of the Roman Catholic Church to the Feminization of Religion." In *Horizons on Catholic Feminist Theology*, eds. Joann Wolski Conn and Walter E. Conn. Washington, D.C.: Georgetown University Press, 1992.

Lefkowitz, Rochelle and Ann Withorn, eds. *For Crying Out Loud: Women and Poverty in the United States.* New York: Pilgrim Press, 1986.

Chapter 1

Cannon, Katie G. and others. *God's Fierce Whimsy.* New York: The Pilgrim Press, 1985.

Carr, Anne. "On Feminist Spirituality." In *Women's Spirituality: Resources for Christian Development*, ed. Joann Wolski Conn. New York: Paulist Press, 1986.

Chung, Hyun-Kyung. *Struggle to Be Sun Again. Maryknoll, New York: Orbis Books, 1990.*

Coles, Robert. *Dorothy Day: A Radical Devotion. Reading, Mass.: Addison-Wesley Pub. Co., 1987.*

Creasy, William. *The Imitation of Christ by Thomas à Kempis: A New Reading of the 1441 Latin Autograph Manuscript.* Macon, Ga.: Mercer University Press, 1989.

Daly, Mary. *Pure Lust: Elemental Feminist Philosophy.* Bos ton: Beacon Press, 1984.

de la Cruz, Sor Juana Inés. *The Answer/La Respuesta.* Translated and edited by Electa Arenal and Amanda Powell. New York: The Feminist Press at the City of University of New York, 1994.

Delmage, Lewis, S.J. *Spiritual Exercises of St. Ignatius Loyola, an American Translation.* New York: Joseph F. Wagner, Inc., 1968.

Diaz-Isasi, Maria and Yolanda Tarango. *Hispanic Women: Prophetic Voice in the Church.* San Francisco: Harper and Row, 1988.

Eugene, Toinette. "Moral Values and Black Womanists." *Journal of Religious Thought* 44 (Winter-Spring 1988).

Falk, Nancy Auer and Rita M. Gross. *Unspoken Worlds: Women's Religious Lives.* Belmont, Ca.: Wadsworth Publishing Co., 1989.

Flinders, Carol Lee. *Enduring Grace: Living Portraits of Seven Women Mystics.* San Francisco: Harper, 1993.

Gardiner, Harold C., S. J., ed. *The Imitation of Christ, Thomas à Kempis: A Modern Version Based on the English Translation Made by Richard Whitford Around the Year 1530.* Garden City, N.Y.: Doubleday, 1955.

Lavrin, Asuncion. "Unlike Sor Juana? The Model Nun in the Religious Literature of Colonial Mexico." In *Feminist Perspectives on Sor Juana Inés de la Cruz,* ed. Stephanie Merrim. Detroit: Wayne State University Press, 1991.

Lorde, Audre. *Sister Outsider: Essays and Speeches.* Trumansburg, N.Y.: Crossing Press, 1984.

Miller, William D. *Dorothy Day.* San Francisco: Harper and Row, 1982.

O'Connor, June E. *The Moral Vision of Dorothy Day: A Feminist Perspective.* New York: Crossroad, 1991.

Ortega, Ofelia, ed. *Women's Visions: Theological Reflection, Celebration, Action.* Geneva, Switzerland: WCC, 1995.

Paulsell, William O. *Tough Minds, Tender Hearts: Six Prophets of Social Justice.* New York: Paulist Press, 1990.

Paz, Octavio. *Sor Juana or the Traps of Faith.* Translated by *Margaret Sayers Peden. Cambridge: Harvard University Press, 1988.*

Russell, Letty and others. *Inheriting our Mothers' Gardens: Feminist Theology in Third World Perspective.* Philadelphia: Westminster Press, 1988.

Sanders, Cheryl J., ed. *Living the Intersection: Womanism and Afrocentrism in Theology. Minneapolis: Fortress* Press, 1995.

Schneiders, Sandra. *Beyond Patching: Faith and Feminism in the Catholic Church.* New York: Paulist Press, 1991.

_____. "Women's Experience and Spirituality." *Spirituality Today* (Summer 1993).

Tavard, George. *Juana Inés de la Cruz and the Theology* of *Beauty: The First Mexican Theology.* Notre Dame: University of Notre Dame Press, 1991.

Thomas à Kempis. *The Imitation of Christ. Translated by E.M. Blaiklock.* Nashville: Thomas Nelson Publishers, 1979.

Walker, Alice. *In Search of Our Mothers' Gardens.* New York: Harcourt Brace, 1983.

Ward, Benedicta, SLG, *Harlots of the Desert.* Kalamazoo: Cistercian Publications, 1987.

_____. *The Sayings of the Desert Fathers.* Kalamazoo: Cistercian Publications, 1975.

Weems, Renita J. *Just a Sister Away: A Womanist Vision of Women's Relationships in the Bible.* San Diego: Lura Media, 1988.

Williams, Delores. *Sisters in the Wilderness: The Challenge of Womanist God-Talk.* Maryknoll, N.Y.: Orbis Books, 1993.

"Women's Congregations That Follow an Ignatian Spirituality: A Report by Jeanne-Françoise de Jaeger." In *Ignatian Spirituality Since CG 32.* Rome, Italy: Centrum Ignatianum Spiritualitatis, n.d.

Chapter 2

Bell, Linda. *Rethinking Ethics in the Midst of Violence.* Boston: Rowman & Littlefield, 1993.

Benhabib, Seyla. "The Generalized and the Concrete Other: The Kohlberg-Gilligan Controversy and Feminist Theory." In *Feminism as Critique*, eds. Seyla Benhabib and Drucilla Cornell. Minneapolis: University of Minneapolis Press, 1987.

Brownmiller, Susan. *Against Our Will: Men, Women and Rape.* New York: Simon and Schuster, 1975.

Daly, Lois K. "Ecofeminism, Reverence for Life, and Feminine Theological Ethics." In *Feminist Theological Ethics,* ed. Lois K. Daly. Louisville: Westminster John Knox Press, 1994.

Daly, Mary. *Gyn/Ecology: The Metaethics of Radical Feminism.* Boston: Beacon Press, 1978.

_____. *Pure Lust: Elemental Feminist Philosophy.* Boston: Beacon Press, 1984.

Farley, Margaret A. "Agape in Feminist Ethics." *Journal of Religious Ethics* 9 (1981).

_____. "Feminist Ethics." In *The Westminster Dictionary of Christian Ethics,* 1986.

_____. "New Patterns of Relationships: Beginnings of a Moral Revolution." *Theological Studies* 36/4 (1975).

Hampson, Daphne. *Theology and Feminism.* Cambridge, Mass.: Basil Blackwell, Inc., 1990.

Haney, Eleanor Humes. "What is Feminist Ethics? A Proposal for Continuing the Discussion." *The Journal of Religious Ethics* 8/1 (Spring 1980).

Harrison, Beverly Wildung. "Theology and Morality of Procreative Choice." In *On Moral Medicine: Theological Perspectives in Medical Ethics*, eds. Stephen E. Lammers and Allen Verhey. Grand Rapids, Mich.: William B. Eerdmans, 1987.

Harrison, Beverly Wildung and Carol S. Robb. *Making the Connections: Essays in Feminist Social Ethics.* Boston: Beacon Press, 1985.

Janeway, Elizabeth. *Powers of the Weak.* New York: William Morrow & Co., Quill Paperbacks, 1981.

Johnson, Elizabeth A. *Women, Earth and Creator Spirit.* New York: Paulist Press, 1993.

Lefkowitz, Rochelle and Ann Withorn, eds. *For Crying Out Loud: Women and Poverty in the United States.* New York: The Pilgrim Press, 1985.

Pagels, Elaine. "The Politics of Paradise: St. Augustine's Exegesis of Genesis 1-3 Versus That of St. John Chrysostom." *Harvard Theological Review* 78:1-2 (1985).

Pateman, Carole. "The Disorder of Women: Women, Love and the Sense of Justice." *Ethics* 91 (October 1980).

Saiving, Valerie. "The Human Situation: A Feminine Viewpoint." *Journal of Religion* 40 (April 1960).

Sanday, Peggy Reeves. *Female Power and Male Dominance: On the Origins of Sexual Inequality.* Cambridge: Cambridge University Press, 1981.

Sölle, Dorothy. *Creative Disobedience.* Cleveland: The Pilgrim Press, 1995.

_____. *Theology for Skeptics.* Minneapolis, Minn.: Fortress Press, 1995.

Tong, Rosemary. *Feminine and Feminist Ethics.* Belmont, Ca.: Wadsworth Publishing Company, 1993.

Welch, Sharon. *A Feminist Ethic of Risk. Minneapolis, Minn.: Fortress Press, 1995.*

Chapter 3

Collins, Mary. "Principles of Feminist Liturgies." In *Women at Worship: Interpretations of North American Diversity,* eds. Marjorie Procter-Smith and Janet R. Walton. Louisville: Westminster/John Knox Press, 1993.

_____. *Worship: Renewal to Practice.* Washington, D.C.: The Pastoral Press, 1987.

Daly, Mary. *Webster's First New Intergalactic Wickedary of the English Language.* Boston: Beacon Press, 1987.

Finn, Peter C. and James M. Schellman, eds. *Shaping English Liturgy: Studies in Honor of Archbishop Denis Hurley.* Washington, D.C.: The Pastoral Press, 1990.

Hilkert, Mary Catherine. "Women Preaching the Gospel." *Theological Digest* 33 (Winter 1986).

Kramarae, Cheris and others, eds. *Language and Power.* Beverly Hills: Sage Publications, 1984.

Lane, Anthony. "Scripture Rescripted: In a New Version Bible Goes P.C." *The New Yorker* (2 October 1995).

Lorde, Audre. "The Transformation of Silence Into Language and Action." In *Sister Outsider: Essays and Speeches.* Trumansburg, N.Y.: Crossing Press, 1984.

_____. "Uses of the Erotic." In *Sister Outsider: Essays and Speeches.* Trumansburg, N.Y.: Crossing Press, 1984.

Morton, Nelle. "The Rising Woman Consciousness in a Male Language Structure." *Andover Newton Quarterly* 12 (March 1972).

Procter-Smith, Marjorie. *In Her Own Rite: Constructing Feminist Liturgical Tradition.* Nashville: Abingdon Press, 1990.

Ramshaw, Gail. *God Beyond Gender: Feminist Christian God Language.* Minneapolis: Fortress Press, 1995.

Raymond, Janice. *A Passion for Friends.* Boston: Beacon Press, 1986.

Rich, Adrienne. *On Lies, Secrets and Silence: Selected Prose, 1966-78.* New York: Norton, 1979.

Ruether, Rosemary Radford. *Women-Church: Theology and Practice of Feminist Liturgical Communities.* San Francisco: Harper and Row, 1985.

Schneiders, Sandra. *Women and the Word.* New York: Paulist Press, 1986.

Schüssler Fiorenza, Elisabeth. *In Memory of Her: A Feminist Theological Reconstruction of Christian Origins.* New York: Crossroad, 1990.

Smith, Christian Marie. *Weaving: A Metaphor and Method for Women's Preaching.* A doctoral dissertation presented to the faculty of the Graduate School of Theology, Berkeley, California. May, 1987.

Spender, Dale. *Man Made Language.* Boston: Routledge & Kegan Paul, 1980.

Thelen, Madonna. *A Threshold for the Spirit: A Feminist Model for Preaching.* A master's thesis presented to the faculty of the Graduate Theological Union. December, 1990.

Thorne, Barrie, Cheris Kramarae, and Nancy Henley. *Language, Gender and Society.* Rowley, Mass.: Newbury House Publishers, Inc., 1983.

Van Leeuwen, Mary Stewart and others. *After Eden: Facing the Challenge of Gender Reconciliation.* Grand Rapids, Mich.: W.B. Eerdmans, 1993.

Chapter 4

Brown, Raymond E. "*Episkope* and *Episkopos*: The New Testament Evidence." *Theological Studies* 41 (1980).

Crosby, Michael. *Celibacy: Means of Control or Mandate of the Heart?* Notre Dame: Ave Maria Press, 1995.

Ewens, Mary, O.P. "Removing the Veil: The Liberated American Nun." In *Women of the Spirit: Female in the Jewish and Christian Traditions,* eds. Rosemary Radford Ruether and Eleanor McLaughlin. New York: Simon and Schuster, 1979.

Heilbrun, Carolyn G. *Writing a Woman's Life.* New York: Ballantine Books, 1988.

Hunt, Mary. "The Challenge of 'Both-And' Theology." In *Women and Church: The Challenge of Ecumenical Solidarity in an Age of Alienation,* ed. Melanie A. May. New York: Friendship Press, 1991.

John Paul II. "On Parishes, Lay Ministry and Women." *Origins* 23:8 (1993): 124-126.

Lacugna, Catherine Mowry. "Catholic Women as Ministers and Theologians." *America* 10 (October 1992): 238-48.

Leege, David C. and Joseph Gremillion, eds. *Notre Dame Study of Catholic Parish Life.* Notre Dame: Notre Dame University Press, 1984-7.

O'Meara, Thomas Franklin. *Theology of Ministry.* New York: Paulist Press, 1983.

Osborne, Kenan, OFM. *Ministry: Lay Ministry in the Roman Catholic Church, Its History and Theology.* New York: Paulist Press, 1993.

Rhodes, Lynn N. *Co-Creating: A Feminist Vision of Ministry.* Philadelphia: Westminster Press, 1987.

Schillebeeckx, Edward. *The Church with a Human Face: A New and Expanded Theology of Ministry.* New York: Crossroad, 1985.

Wallace, Ruth. *They Call Her Pastor: A New Role for Catholic Women.* Albany, N.Y.: SUNY Press, 1992.

Weaver, Mary Jo. *New Catholic Women.* San Francisco: Harper and Row, 1985.

Wittberg, Patricia, S.C. "Non-ordained Workers in the Catholic Church: Power and Mobility Among American Nuns." *Journal for the Scientific Study of Religion* 28, (June 1989): 148-61.

Chapter 5

Atwood, Margaret. *Good Bones and Simple Murders.* New York: Doubleday, 1994.

Bateson, Mary Catherine. *Composing a Life.* New York: Penguin Books, Plume Edition, 1990.

Boff, Leonardo. *Church: Charism and Power, Liberation Theology and the Institutional Church.* Translated by John W. Diercksmeier. New York: Crossroad, 1985.

Chittister, Joan. *Job's Daughters: Women and Power.* New York: Paulist Press, 1990.

Darling, Pamela W. *New Wine: The Story of Women Transforming Leadership and Power in the Episcopal Church.* Boston: Cowling Publications, 1994.

Dinnerstein, Dorothy. *The Mermaid and the Minotaur: Sexual Arrangements and Human Malaise.* New York: Harper and Row, 1976.

Endo, Shusaku. The Samurai. Translated by Van C. Gessel. New York: Vintage Books, 1984.

"Equal is as Equal Does." *Women-Convergence,* 1995.

Heilbrun, Carolyn G. *Writing a Woman's Life*. New York: Ballantine Books, 1988.

Lorde, Audre. "A New Spelling of Our Name." In *Front Line Feminism, 1975-1995: Essays from Sojourner's First 20 Years*, ed. Karen Kahn. San Francisco: Aunt Lute Books, 1995.

Milhaven, Annie Lally, ed. *The Inside Stories: 13 Valiant Women Challenging the Church*. Mystic, Conn.: Twenty-Third Publications, 1987.

Ruether, Rosemary Radford. *Women-Church: Theology and Practice of Feminist Liturgical Communities*. San Francisco: Harper and Row, 1985.

Russell, Letty. *Household of Freedom: Authority in Feminist Theology*. Philadelphia: The Westminster Press, 1987.

Sturtz, Ronald E. *The Guitar of God: Gender, Power, and Authority in the Visionary World of Mother Juana de la Cruz (1481-1534)*. Philadelphia: University of Pennsylvania Press, 1990.

Wheatley, Margaret J. *Leadership and the New Science: Learning About Organization from an Orderly Universe*. San Francisco: Berrett-Koehler Publications, 1994.

Conclusion

Katzenstein, Mary Fainsod. "Discursive Politics and Feminist Activism in the Catholic Church." In *Feminist Organizations: Harvest of the New Women's Movement*, eds. Myra Marx Ferree and Patricia Yancey Martin. Philadelphia: Temple University Press, 1995.